THE
WICHITA
LINEMAN

Dylan Jones studied at Chelsea School of Art and St Martin's School of Art. A former editor at *i-D*, *The Face*, *Arena*, the *Observer* and the *Sunday Times*, he is currently the Editor-in-Chief of *GQ*. Under his editorship, the magazine has won over fifty awards. He is the author of the *Sunday Times* bestseller *David Bowie: A Life* and the *New York Times* bestseller *Jim Morrison: Dark Star*. A trustee of the Hay Festival, in 2013 he was awarded an OBE for services to publishing.

Further praise for *The Wichita Lineman*:

'Author and *GQ* editor Dylan Jones builds a worthy case . . . balancing insight from the record's creators with its influence on American culture and personal reflections on its artistry.' Peter Blackstock, *Financial Times*

'If you're going to craft an entire book around one song, then it would have to be something like Glen Campbell's

1968 masterpiece "Wichita Lineman".' *Hot Press*, Music Book of the Fortnight

'Jones shows how it subtly highlights the drama singing through the wires.' *Uncut*

'Jones, via deep-digging, biography, interviews, social history and travelogue, gets under the skin of exactly why – specifically as conveyed by Glen Campbell – it has attained an invincible classic status.' *Irish Times*

'Jones's affection for Webb and Campbell and his easy-worn knowledge of the details of their lives and songs is infectious and engrossing.' *RTÉ*

'Dylan writes avidly and draws extensively from interviews with all the key players, as well as from his own memories of hearing the song in his own home.' *Shindig!*

'This excellent book goes some way towards shifting attention back to [Glen Campbell's] finest years . . . It's impossible not to recognise the lush, lavish simplicity of this poetry.' *R2*

'Book of the week.' *London Review of Books*

'Satisfies without a wasted word.' *Kirkus*

'Encompasses life in the heartland and L.A.'s booming 1960s music industry.' *Los Angeles Times*

THE
WICHITA
LINEMAN

SEARCHING IN THE SUN
FOR THE WORLD'S GREATEST
UNFINISHED SONG

DYLAN JONES

faber

First published in 2019
by Faber & Faber Limited
Bloomsbury House
74–77 Great Russell Street
London WC1B 3DA

This paperback edition published in 2020

First published in the USA in 2019

Typeset by Faber & Faber Limited
Printed and bound by CPI Group (UK) Ltd, Croydon CRO 4YY

A CIP record for this book
is available from the British Library

ISBN 978-0-571-35341-5

10 9 8 7 6 5 4 3 2 1

For Louis

CONTENTS

I think it's prima facie evidence for the existence of God because for me to grow up and actually end up working with Glen Campbell is almost unbelievable.

JIMMY WEBB

PREFACE: MY FATHER'S PLACE

When I play it's mostly music, but
there's a real demand for stories.
I started doing it almost fearfully.
I began playing maybe fifteen
songs, and doing some stories.
Over the last ten years, I've got to
remember to play ten songs, with
more stories, and the audiences
seem to love it.

JIMMY WEBB

Once upon a time, Long Island was a very particular musical laboratory, the place you came to witness the latest cell division of rock and roll. If you lived on Long Island in the seventies and someone said, 'Meet me tonight in dreamland,' there was only one thing you were going to do, only one place you were going to go.

Back then, if you needed any litmus test as to who was about to cut through, wanted to find out which heavily touted newbie actually had real talent, you went to My Father's Place, a 7,000-square-foot cabaret club in Roslyn, a historic village up in Nassau County. U2 made their American debut here; in 1976, it was where the Ramones performed their most important out-of-town dates; and back in 1973, an aspiring Bruce Springsteen performed here to just thirty people. He loved the place so much he came back four more times, even after he became more famous than the club ever would be. Here, twenty-two miles from Manhattan, up-and-coming comedians like Eddie Murphy, Andy Kaufman and Billy Crystal made their starts. In an era when comedy and rock went hand in hand, if you wanted to break into either industry, My Father's Place was where you came.

In the fifteen years before the club closed in 1987, My Father's Place hosted more than six thousand shows by over three thousand acts. The club's owner, Michael 'Eppy' Epstein, refused to book cover bands, and so the club became known as somewhere aspiring artists could perform. Billy Joel. Todd Rundgren. Madonna. Aerosmith. Along with CBGBs and Max's Kansas City, the club became a nurturing ground for proto-punk and new-wave bands such as Iggy and the Stooges, the New York Dolls, the Runaways, the Police, Blondie, Talking Heads and Television.

Early in 2018, Epstein reopened the club not far from the original venue, in the basement of the newly renovated Roslyn Hotel (formerly the Roslyn Claremont Hotel, but now reimagined as a boutique country inn), and six months later, in October, I came to have a look myself, or rather I came to see Jimmy Webb. Even though he lives not far from it, this was the first time he'd played the new venue, and it was something of a big deal for him. Webb regularly plays in New York, in London, in Sydney, all over the world. But there's nothing like playing in your own backyard.

The Roslyn is a rather unprepossessing place that reminded me in part of one of those resort hotels in the Catskill mountains (albeit somewhat smaller). The surrounding area is generic middle-class America; not full of the Oklahoman homesteads of Jimmy Webb's childhood, but instead the kind of white clapboard homes that pepper this section of Long Island in the same way that swimming pools litter certain parts of Los Angeles. If you ever wanted to see the houses and hoses and sprinklers on the lawn that Richard Harris invoked in 'The Yard Went On

Forever', one of the ferociously eccentric songs that Jimmy Webb wrote for the actor in 1968 – the same year he wrote 'Wichita Lineman' for Glen Campbell – they are here, in this white-bread enclave of Oyster Bay.

The basement looked as though it had played host to a succession of wedding receptions, birthdays and hen parties, with its pink neon, wood panelling, turquoise ruched drapes and jellyfish chandeliers. Webb's performance was a brunch gig, and the menu in the club reflected this: mimosas, chicken paillard Caesar salad and eggs Benedict; popcorn dipped in truffle, black pepper and Parmesan; lollipop wings, pickles, candied nuts and kimchee. Plus, of course, the obligatory lemon ricotta pancakes with smoked salmon and Chardonnay – a signature combo here.

Ashley, my server for the afternoon, having ascertained that I was from London told me enthusiastically that her father was originally from Sheffield, the unspoken assumption being that of course I had probably met him at some point. Such is the eternal optimism of the second-generation immigrant.

There were two hundred people in the club, all of whom had made a small pilgrimage to see the man known as America's Songwriter, a man responsible for some of the greatest popular songs of the twentieth century, the Midwestern genius who wrote 'Wichita Lineman', 'By the Time I Get to Phoenix' and 'MacArthur Park', the man who, in the space of a few months in the summer of 1968, became the most famous songwriter in America. All for $50 plus lunch.

I hadn't seen him perform since 1994, when, for three weeks in September, Webb, then a sprightly forty-eight, had given Londoners a chance to experience his voice in person for the first time in over a decade. The Café Royal's Green Room had been operating as a supper-club venue for just over a year, hosting small, personal concerts by the likes of Eartha Kitt, Michael Feinstein and Sacha Distel, where dinner and cabaret would set you back £48 per person. Even at this point in his career, Webb was obviously an old hand at cabaret, making a point of trying to build a Vegas-style rapport with the audience from the first song in. There were small jokes, polished witty asides and plenty of music-industry anecdotes. A tall man, he spent most of the concert crouched over his keyboards, his ponytail bouncing behind him, with his eyes shut and his head pointing heavenwards, as if leaning towards divine inspiration. He began with an uplifting version of 'Up, Up and Away', before leaving the sixties behind and addressing 'The Highwayman', 'Still Within the Sound of Your Voice' and 'The Moon's a Harsh Mistress'. *Rolling Stone* once said that Webb has a voice like an old Mustang, but there were times during the evening at the Café Royal when the car appeared to be running on empty. And yet he ploughed on: 'Didn't We', 'If These Walls Could Speak' and 'MacArthur Park' were followed by an obligatory medley of 'By the Time I Get to Phoenix', 'Galveston' and the pearl of the evening, 'Wichita Lineman'. Here, finally, was a moment of genuine beauty, when Webb's compassion and latent melancholia seemed to overshadow any inadequacies he may have had as a vocalist, causing ripples and fleeting epiphanies all over the Café Royal.

In Roslyn, there was a low-level buzz in the audience; not feverish anticipation, but something altogether more nuanced. The people gathered here today had come to see a man they'd often read about, but whom most had never seen, making Webb something of an enigma. At the meet and greet afterwards he was (discreetly) mobbed by people saying how great it was to finally meet the man who wrote these wonderful songs and hear him sing them in person. The audience had come to hear the songs as much as they'd come to see Jimmy Webb. After all, in the sixties, these tunes helped build a new kind of America, tunes that for many defined a generation. 'I never got to hear Berlin or Gershwin perform in a club, however, I will be able to say I saw Jimmy Webb sitting at a Steinway . . . performing his songs,' said Stephen Sorokoff of the *Times Square Chronicles*. 'Words and Music that are embedded in the musical soul of our country, and will be played for generations to come. I hope it's not too over the top to say, but for the non-music lovers out there, I can only compare it to hearing Thomas Jefferson reading the Declaration of Independence . . .' Webb has other fans, too. 'At an age when other singers are losing their voices, Mr Webb finds his mercurial, unguarded singing . . . attaining the gritty authority of a soft-hearted country outlaw's,' wrote Stephen Holden in the *New York Times*.

After the servers finished gathering the plates and glasses in the basement, it was suddenly show time. The lights dimmed, and Webb, dressed entirely in security-guard black, walked quickly through the audience and straight away sat behind the black Yamaha grand, before adjusting his microphone and beaming at the crowd. The applause kept going until he reached the stage, but even if it hadn't, I can't imagine he would have felt slighted, because what Jimmy Webb has in spades is confidence. Not arrogance, but a Midwestern confidence that is immediately infectious. Happy in himself and comfortable in his skin, he almost seemed oblivious to his surroundings, and gave the impression he'd actually behave the same if he were playing Carnegie Hall this afternoon rather than a glorified supper club in Nassau County.

And then he started, methodically making his way through his extraordinary collection of hits, an eclectic bunch of songs that are among the most successful ever recorded. Every time he got a hint of recognition from the crowd – and as so many of his songs are famous this happened every time his fingers returned to the piano – he smiled a big Liberace-type Midwestern smile of genuine warmth, demonstrating a little bit of old-school Vegas on Long Island's North Shore.

The crowd was completely smitten, which makes any criticism of his vocal abilities seem rather churlish. Would they have applauded any more enthusiastically if he'd hit every one of the notes he'd missed? Unlikely. Impossible, actually. Could they have been any more rapturous in their appreciation if he'd been rather less approximate with his interpretation? I wouldn't have imagined so.

Every night Jimmy Webb seems to get away with it, singing these famous songs he invented with as much passion and pathos as he probably did when he first wrote them; maybe with more, actually, as the songs have had time to wrap themselves in the misfortunes of experience. This afternoon he sort of slid his way through his tunes – almost walking–talking them like Burt Bacharach does – interrupting them with well-worn stories that mentioned everyone from Frank Sinatra and Richard Harris to Billy Joel and Kanye West, the somewhat legendary session guitarist Carol Kaye and, of course, his dear departed 'brother', Glen Campbell. He has become self-deprecating about his voice – 'They don't pay me as much when I sing,' he joked to the audience – and on a few of the songs he asked the crowd to join in on some of the tougher passages. Of course, what this meant was that today a further two hundred people could claim to have sung a song with Jimmy Webb.

By the time he got to 'Wichita Lineman', however, Webb's voice had settled down to the extent that he performed it almost perfectly. Almost beautifully, in fact. Just like he'd done a quarter of a century ago in London. He has never had the pipes his partner Glen Campbell had, but this afternoon Webb's interpretation of his greatest song was just about as good as it could be, given the circumstances (the primary circumstance being the fact that the man who

wrote it had just celebrated his seventy-second birthday).
And as he carefully slowed the song down – moving down
through the gears – the piano keys started mimicking the
Morse code refrain that has always signalled the song's
finale, Webb's fingers delicately tinkling over the horizon.
This was close to a faultless performance, with Webb reaching for notes with his body as much as his voice.

Then, after ninety minutes, he was gone, replaced by the
piped strains of Miles Davis's *Kind of Blue* pouring out of the
house PA, and scooting off to the lobby for the obligatory
photographs and CD and book signing. He was effortlessly
charming with those who queued for the merchandise, and
no smile, no handshake, no awkward selfie appeared to be
too much trouble. The night before I had seen his fellow My
Father's Place alumnus Bruce Springsteen perform his one-
man show at the 960-seat Walter Kerr theatre on Broadway,
and it wasn't just their stagecraft that was so similar, it was
also the affection they showed the audience, ever mindful of
who pays the ferryman.

There were two parts of Springsteen's show that were
particularly revealing: one that grabbed you almost before
you'd sat down, as he spent the first five minutes of the
show self-deprecatingly demolishing any right he may have
had to represent the working man; and then, conveniently,
just before the end of the evening, when he talked about the
two central motivations that seem to propel all performers
– namely the desire to leave home and explore new lands,
and then, inevitably, the unnecessarily tortuous search for a

way back. It's said of the US that the further west you go, the more there is of nothing, and in many respects that's one of the country's greatest metaphors. Home: it's what the search for success is all about.

Jimmy Webb was in a similarly reflective mood this afternoon, riffing on his own Faustian bargain. 'I suppose when I was young my mother had made a contract with me,' he said, smiling at his audience. 'I would play piano for an hour a day and she wouldn't hit me with a stick. That was the contract. It was simple, really. And when I started improvising on my piano I seriously thought I could make something of it. And it worked. By the time I was twenty all my dreams had come true. I was a farmer's boy who was now living in California, in Hollywood. I had a big house, lots of cars ... but something wasn't quite right.'

The crowd was suddenly restless, unsure as to what was going to happen next, perhaps worried that their Sunday afternoon might be veering off into sadness. 'I was stuck in the middle, being a traditional songwriter in one way, and a kind of pretend hippie in another. And I wasn't accepted by either ... So the only thing I could do was continue to write my songs ...'

And then his fingers hit the keys again, and all was right with the world. At least up in Roslyn.

The night before, he had played a gig up in Purchase, in Westchester County, and after a fairly punishing touring schedule involving performances all over Europe and the US, he was happy to be playing places where he could drive home afterwards. For the last fifteen years or so he has lived in Bayville, on Long Island Sound, and he likes to look at the seagulls and the ospreys as he walks along the beach with his second wife, and manager, Laura. Laura's mother was sitting next to me in the club, and she could not have been happier with her son-in-law's performance, and seemed equally pleased with his appearance in that day's *Newsday*. 'Isn't that wonderful?' she asked rhetorically, showing me her copy.

A few weeks after this performance, Webb would be inducted into the Long Island Music Hall of Fame, something which pleased him no end, and which he was looking forward to enormously. 'This is just totally unexpected,' he said to the crowd. 'I have attended a couple of the ceremonies and I was there once to induct Johnny Maestro and the Brooklyn Bridge [Webb wrote their 1968 hit "The Worst That Could Happen"], so I've been around the proceedings. But I never foresaw being inducted myself.'

On stage in Roslyn, he was also full of appreciation for being allowed to play on such hallowed soil. 'This is such an iconic club, and when I think of all the great people who have played here, I'm humbled.' He said he hoped that his performance would help 'further embed myself into the Long Island zeitgeist', but then said that he was sure the only reason he's accepted here on Long Island is because he lives down the street from Billy Joel.

Over the next few months the Roslyn would also play host to Black Uhuru, Gary U.S. Bonds, Randy Jackson, the

Tubes, Steve Forbert, Billy J. Kramer, Brand X and Bettye LaVette, a perfect example of the eclectic democratisation of the modern club circuit in a world where musicians can't make money from record sales any more. Few of them would have the emotional pull of Jimmy Webb, however; few of them would be able to perform songs that continually offer such connection and transcendence.

This afternoon, before he started gearing up for the emotional denouement of 'Wichita Lineman', Webb told the story of how one of his sons came to him a few years ago and told him a song of his was on the radio. Not one of his classics, though, but a new version of something he'd written fifty years previously. The song his son had heard was Kanye West's 'Famous', which contained a substantial sample of Nina Simone's 1968 recording of Webb's song 'Do What You Gotta Do'.

'So I listen to this record, and apart from the fact that Kanye West is saying some pretty repugnant things about Taylor Swift, this was basically my song with a lot of rapping over the top,' said Webb. 'I have to tell you I was quite upset. But my publisher eventually sorted it out, not that he knew anything about it when I called him to complain about it. But he called me one day to tell me he'd managed to get me 45 per cent of the publishing. And so I thought to myself, "Well, Taylor's a big girl."'

As the audience erupted with laughter, Webb peeled off another anecdote, this one involving Art Garfunkel and Frank Sinatra (or Mr Sinatra, as Webb still calls him). There would be many other stories, many other tales involving Willie Nelson, Elvis Presley, the Beatles, the Rolling Stones, Linda Ronstadt, Waylon Jennings, Glen Campbell and, of course, 'Wichita Lineman', which might just be the best story of all.

Life is long and songs are short, though 'Wichita Lineman' manages to squeeze a lifetime of emotion into just three minutes, and the story of how it came to be, how it was written, assembled and produced is one of the most intriguing in all of pop. This Midwestern small-town song would flood our psyche and make us feel alive, ignoring gravity as it carried us all up into the sky above the Kansas–Oklahoma border.

'I'm surprised really because it was such a simple little thing,' said Webb, when I asked him if he understood why so many people think 'Wichita Lineman' is the best song ever recorded. 'But I'm aware of people's feelings towards it, to some degree. It still sounds great today . . .'

INTRODUCTION:
THE SLEEPER

Ars est celare artem.
(True art is to conceal art.)

For many years I thought I was the only person who liked Glen Campbell's 'Wichita Lineman'; in truth I thought I was the only person from my generation who might have heard of it, let alone actually listened to the record. The song was as much a part of my childhood as the other records my parents filled the house with, and along with Dean Martin, Frank Sinatra and Matt Monro, the work of Glen Campbell saturated my life. Actually, to be more accurate, it saturated my parents' life. I just happened to be there at the time.

I wish I could remember where I was when I first heard it, I really do, but nothing bubbles up. It was just one of those songs that was always around, like the others my parents often played at home by Sinatra, Martin, folk singer Bob ('Elusive Butterfly') Lind, country star Roger Miller, one-hit wonders Esther and Abi Ofarim ('Cinderella Rockefella'), the Seekers (lots and lots of them, from 'The Carnival Is Over' and 'Georgy Girl' to 'I'll Never Find Another You' and, my favourite, 'A World of Our Own') and Dutch calypso duo Nina and Frederik. Actually, I think these were probably my mother's records. Her favourite, Dean, blasted daily through the walls, and as I heard her singing along, even as a boy I could tell she wasn't really happy, and that she was singing about a world that would

17

never be within her reach, resigned instead to a life of compromise and domesticity. How she semaphored this, I don't know, but even when she was happily singing, her sadness appeared to define her. You pick things up as a kid. Especially when your parents are always fighting.

'Ah, Dino,' she would say emphatically, as though she were wistfully remembering some romantic Sorrento holiday. 'What an old smoothie.'

She was being dismissive while at the same time taking a kind of ownership of him, but even she couldn't disguise the fact that she obviously found him completely exotic. Imagine! She owned not one Dean Martin record but several! Back in the sixties, to my parents' generation, buying a new record – be it single, EP or album – wasn't incidental, it wasn't like buying a pack of cigarettes. It was like buying a fridge or a television set. I can still remember my mother saying to my father, on more than one occasion, 'Shall we listen to the new Dean Martin record again?'

Swells, she called them, when she mentioned Dean and Frank, and that's what they were – swells.

These were the first pieces of vinyl I ever remember holding, racked in a vinyl-coated dark-green box – with a cheap, goldish metal lock on the lid – just big enough to hold about forty seven-inch singles. There were all sorts of singles in there, mostly in thin, brightly coloured paper sleeves, and all looking as though they'd been imported from America. I've still got my parents' beautifully scratched 45 of John Barry's wistful 'Vendetta', still got an EP of various tracks from *Songs for Swinging Lovers*, still got Topol's 'If I Were a Rich Man' (from the 1964 musical *Fiddler on the Roof*). There was lots of Herb Alpert, too, and if history can be caught in a single breath, then there are few better ways of explaining the populuxe aspirations of American suburbia during the late fifties and early sixties (when the advertising industry began to believe its own publicity) than by listening to the piercing yet sweet 'Ameriachi' sound of Alpert and his Tijuana Brass.

These were largely American tastes, but then at home we were steeped in Americana. Not only that, we almost *felt* American.

Lying around the house also was a record by Les Baxter, the soundtrack composer who, along with Martin Denny and Arthur Lyman, helped invent the hyper-world of exotica. How esoteric of my parents. Baxter excelled at space-age bachelor-pad music, creating enchanting little symphonies that conjured up exotic images of the Gold Coast, the South Pacific, the Andes, even other planets.

Home for me was rather less exotic, namely a bungalow in a small Norfolk village, an overspill community from the local US Air Force base, which was full of American pilots and their beehived wives, who all appeared to wear pedal-pushers, stilettos and completely opaque Jackie O shades (the wives, not the pilots). Even when they were picking up their children from the local school. I spent much of my childhood on air-force bases, both British and American, so I suppose it's no surprise that from an early age I latched on to the obvious manifestations of US pop culture – food, clothes, cars and the records of Dean Martin. From England's 1966 World Cup victory through to the moon landing in 1969, Martin was rarely off our turntable, and many of my early memories revolve around listening to 'Return to Me', 'Volare', 'Under the Bridges of Paris', 'You Belong to Me' and 'Napoli'. For me, these songs were gaudily exotic but homely at the same time, and defined a certain kind of sophistication, no matter how ersatz it may have been.

I would stare at those Dean Martin singles for hours. They all had heavily stylised photographs of him on the picture sleeves (which, even back then, were so brittle they were in danger of cracking). Martin was a hypnotically attractive figure, even though he himself was as unself-conscious as a performer could be. Dean Martin looked like he swung not just because swinging was cool, but because it was easy. And Dean Martin was nothing if not easy. His singing style was practically weightless; disdaining obvious effort and explicit emotional involvement, it suggested the detachment of a new kind of hipster. When he sang, Dino unfolded with an exaggerated smirk, an effortless shrug of the shoulders. These impressions would gather momentum as I got older, but even as a boy I found him quite fascinating. I would, wouldn't I, if my mother liked him so much?

It wasn't just the music, of course. It never was. The man pictured on the single, EP and LP sleeves lying around the house was like no man I had ever seen; you didn't get many Italian-Americans swanning around East Anglia dressed in herringbone sports jackets, butterfly-collared shirts and polka-dot cravats. And certainly not in pink V-neck cardigans, white silk socks and black suede loafers. Not even on the US Air Force bases where I grew up. But then that was the point, I guess. Dino inhabited a world that wasn't easily accessible to an eight-year-old who was yet to buy his own trousers, let alone visit the Sahara Tahoe.

Other obsessions would soon occur – the Beach Boys, followed in quick succession by David Bowie, Steely Dan, Tom Wolfe and the Ramones – but I never forgot the slightly louche, debonair gadabout who sang like an angel and dressed like a gangster on his day off. Soon enough I realised that Dino wasn't alone in his sartorial elegance, and after discovering Frank Sinatra – with his club bow tie and straw hat – and the rest of the Rat Pack (Sammy Davis Jr, Peter Lawford and Joey Bishop), perhaps unsurprisingly I became quietly obsessed with fifties and sixties Americana.

In tandem with this, I started to develop a completely unironic taste for the loungecore torch song, although in those days it was known by the rather more prosaic moniker of 'middle of the road ballad' – particularly those sung by Glen Campbell. His image was slightly more confusing, as he looked like someone pretending to be a cowboy. If I stared at the cover of the *Wichita Lineman* album long enough (and the ability of teenage and pre-teen boys in the sixties and seventies to stare at record sleeves was quite phenomenal; I've often thought that if I had adhered to Malcolm Gladwell's famous 10,000-hour rule and spent four hundred days doing something else, I could have become a champion chess player, Tour de France cyclist or concert pianist), I came away thinking that the man on the front didn't really match the man singing the songs. He was wearing a brown suede jacket, a red polka-dot shirt (the kind of thing that Dean Martin may have been able to get away with), clinically parted hair, bright white teeth and a pleasing down-home smile.

For me there was far too much optimism going on here.

I eventually worked out that 'Wichita Lineman', like most of Glen Campbell's great songs, had not been written by Campbell himself, but by somebody called Jimmy Webb, someone who someone else had called the Master of Sad – the author of terrifically maudlin songs such as 'By the Time I Get to Phoenix', 'Where's the Playground, Susie?', 'Galveston', etc. (Campbell called the songs 'hurt soul'). If you read reports written at the time of Campbell and Webb's alliance, you'll see that this was meant to be a great crossover marriage, the maverick pop composer consorting with the clean-cut country singer, the Democrat cavorting with the Republican, as though some gigantic sociological barrier had just been bridged. This was the harmonising of America. At first glance they certainly looked like different people, and Jimmy Webb didn't seem to smile as much in his photographs. Their partnership, however, would turn out to be alchemic, as enthralling an alliance between writer and singer as has ever been achieved in popular music.

In anyone else's hands, 'Wichita Lineman' could have

been overly sentimental and somewhat odd. The idea of a telephone repair man listening to, and falling in love with, a woman singing down a phone line – if indeed that's what she was doing – is bizarre, to say the least, and not the sort of thing you could have imagined Frank Sinatra warming to. But in Glen Campbell's hands it became such an evocation that it had middle America enraptured.

Later, looking deeper, I discovered Campbell had played guitar on the Beach Boys' *Pet Sounds*, recorded the little-known Brian Wilson classic 'Guess I'm Dumb', and that he had played the guitar himself on 'Lineman', on a Danelectro six-string bass. As I got older, I became even more intrigued by 'Lineman', reading as much about it as I could find – which, pre-Internet, wasn't much. I sought out Jimmy Webb concerts and Glen Campbell concerts, and once even wrote a piece about the provenance of the song for the *Independent*. As a teenager it was one of those records I listened to when I wanted to feel sad. Seriously, if you wanted to feel sorry for yourself, then 'Wichita Lineman' was the way to go. I would spontaneously start singing it as I was walking down the street, or when I was in the pub, or – later – even at dinner parties, much to my wife's horror. There were other songs I loved, but few that managed to pull me up like this one. I loved 'Beyond the Sea' by Bobby Darin (an English interpretation of 'La Mer' by Charles Trenet), 'On Days Like These' by Matt Monro (the theme from *The Italian Job*), 'Diamonds Are Forever' by Shirley Bassey (the second of her three James Bond themes) – all of them rather morose, plaintive songs, albeit with terrific melodies – but none of them had the ability to lift or tear me up like 'Wichita Lineman'.

It was when I started researching the song that I found out – shock, deep shock – that it was actually unfinished, and that Jimmy Webb had never intended it to be recorded or released in this form.

It was the perfect imperfect song.

One of the reasons I liked the record so much was because it didn't really sound like anything else. Even in those years when I first started hearing it, and before I started to develop a typical schoolboy (and rather granular) obsession with genre and taste, I thought there was something odd about it. Something fundamentally different. It wasn't a traditional pop song, wasn't rock and wasn't your usual cornball country. I suppose in essence it's a great *We've-Gotta-Get-Outta-This-Place*-type song, a record that manages to articulate our desire to be somewhere else, to inhabit another life, even though it celebrates the everyday. I think another reason I liked it was because I figured no one else could assert ownership of it. Far from being concerned with the bridging of distance to find a tribe, in this particular case I was proactively seeking isolation. This wasn't teenage one-upmanship; I wasn't trying to be esoteric, wasn't trying to impress my friends with a record they'd never heard of, but I'm sure part of my fondness for it stemmed from me being fairly sure that no one else my age would feel the same way about it.

The older I got, the more I realised how wrong I was.

Apparently, or so it seemed, there were dozens of people I knew who liked it, and just as many who appeared to be as obsessive as I was about it, and who appeared to venerate it as much as I did. Bob Dylan once even said it was the greatest song ever written. 'The song's so enthralling as it's a mystery,' journalist and magazine guru Mark Ellen told me. 'As you know, Jimmy Webb had sent off a rough version to Glen Campbell, and Campbell recorded it as it was. That's partly why it's so intriguing, as it's unfinished and it doesn't explain itself. You have no real idea what it's about. I was fourteen when it came out and thought a lineman was a railroad worker mending the railway lines. It didn't matter. The song paints a vague picture of a barren landscape and longing and loneliness. It's like a pencil sketch, and you fill in the colours yourself.'

I think we all had a suspicion that there was a hidden, deeper meaning contained within it, a metaphor perhaps. But there appeared to be no irony involved in the construction and performance of the song, and it wasn't as though this was in any way a cogent satire on American society ... so what could it be? And then I figured that the reason we probably all liked it so much was because of its simplicity, its transparency and its honesty. There was no metaphor here, only the plaintive extrapolation of a universal truth.

A relatively simple tale of a lonely telephone repair man diligently working in the vast open plains of the American Midwest, 'Wichita Lineman' is the first existential country song. It's also probably the greatest existential torch song ever written. Whereas a lot of pop holds the world at a prophylactic remove, 'Wichita' is not only subtly engaging, but after listening to it repeatedly you get a sense that the subtext of the song contemplates what it might mean to find transcendence in such work. And it only takes two minutes and fifty-eight seconds to do so.

'Up close by the Kansas border and the Panhandle of Oklahoma there's a place where the terrain absolutely flattens out,' said Jimmy Webb, who as a boy travelled those roads in his father's car. 'It's almost like you could take a [spirit] level out of your toolkit and put it on the highway and that bubble would just sit right there on dead centre, and it goes on that way for about fifty miles, in the heat of summer with the heat rising off the road in this kind of shimmering mirage, the telephone poles gradually materialising out of this far, distant perspective, becoming larger and then rushing towards you.'

Jimmy Webb's memory is foolproof.

'It was when I was in High School, and I was fifteen or sixteen. I was in my dad's car, and I suddenly looked up at one of these telephone poles and there was a man on top of it, talking on the telephone, and he was gone very quickly, and I had another twenty-five miles of absolute solitude to meditate on this apparition. It was a splendidly vivid, cinematic image that I lifted out of my deep memory while I was writing this song about an ordinary guy.'

It was all about the silhouette. Webb could see him on top of this pole talking or listening or doing something with the telephone. For some reason, the starkness of the image stayed with him like a photograph. Later, when he was trying to write the song, he imagined what his narrator would say if he picked up the telephone there and then.

And then Glen Campbell sings those immortal words: 'And I need you more than want you / and I want you for all time . . .'

Fifteen words that manage to capture the salient emotion of every teary ballad that ever plucked your heart strings, a couplet that can break, mend or hold your heart in under ten seconds, a handful of words that, as the critic and broadcaster Mark Steyn pointed out, echo those lines in the old Hollywood show tune 'Stranger in Paradise', where someone hangs suspended in space, until they know that there might be a chance that someone cares.

'What I was really trying to say was, you can see someone working in construction or working in a field, a migrant worker or a truck driver, and you may think you know what's going on inside him, but you don't,' said Webb. 'You can't assume that a man isn't a poet. And that's really what the song is about.'

This wasn't music that strode out of the shadows like the opening credits of a spaghetti western; no, this was music that meandered into view, hovering in the middle of the lawn and hissing like a sprinkler.

'Wichita Lineman' was not *of the moment*. It might have been a bit melodramatic, and yet the record didn't announce itself with any great fanfare. It didn't capture the zeitgeist.

27

How could it? 'Like a Rolling Stone', for example, which had been released three years earlier, was epochal, and as soon as it hit the radio, lives began to change, and culture started to churn. Nothing similar was expected of 'Wichita Lineman', as it snuck out without much ambition, other than some hoped-for commercial success. It stretched outside the confines of country radio for sure, but it would take years for the song to become the phenomenon it is now and find its resonance.

At the time, 'Wichita Lineman' went largely unnoticed, as it appeared in the midst of a world still grappling with the transitional tropes of the counter-culture. When you had a generation espousing 'Make Love Not War', who was going to notice a quirky and overly melodramatic country tune about a telephone repair man? If *Sgt. Pepper's Lonely Hearts Club Band* was all about 'Beethoven coming to the supermarket' (in the words of the arch Yippie Abbie Hoffman), then Jimmy Webb's opus was surely just about the prairie coming to the radio.

To those who were taking notice, the song may have appeared to be slightly strange, although any idiosyncrasies harboured by 'Wichita Lineman' would surely have been obscured by the knowledge that the man singing it on the radio had previously been responsible for two hit records that – on the surface at least – seemed to be archetypes of contemporary country pop: 'Gentle on My Mind' and 'By the Time I Get to Phoenix' (which had actually been written by Webb himself). Webb's song may have been about the harvesting of emotion rather than the dignity of labour, but it couldn't compare to songs about dancing or fighting in the streets, or to the media attention being focused on the denouement of a decade seemingly dedicated to all forms of cultural insurrection, however randomly it may have manifested itself.

With the iconic songs of the sixties it was all about immediacy. They were launched, and they landed. 'Like a Rolling Stone' had it, as did 'Satisfaction', 'Substitute', Jimi Hendrix's version of 'All Along the Watchtower'. The moment they existed, the moment became theirs. They owned it. 'Wichita Lineman', however, was insidious. It was a sleeper. Stealthily, like a Paul Weller ballad, a Donald Fagen key change or a Prefab Sprout harmony, the song crept up on you, snaking around the brow of the hill rather than careering over the top accompanied by five thousand strong men with muskets and spears. Like Woody Allen's Zelig, one day it was suddenly there, never to disappear. Then it was everywhere, for ever. On the radio, on the television, on the mix tape, on the B-side, cropping up as the unlikely encore. (When you don't have a dog, they're invisible; when you get one, you see them everywhere, even in your dreams.)

That, for me, is 'Wichita Lineman', a song I heard as a boy that has stayed with me all my life. I like it now for the same reasons I liked it then. I liked it because it took me to places I hadn't been; to places nowhere near me, places unknown. It was a complete escape. It may have been a song full of longing, full of anxiety and want, yet to me it seemed to announce a vortex of calm.

I am not the only one who cannot recall when they first heard it; no one else can either. They may have been aware of it during a formative period of their life, but I've yet to meet anyone who can remember precisely where they were when they first heard it, or when it was. The song was just around. 'That's the thing about "Wichita Lineman",' said a friend of mine, when I told him I was writing a book about it. 'You don't know when you first heard it, as it was just one of those songs from your childhood that was sort of always there. It was always there in the background, being there. I suppose I remember it always being there, although it obviously can't have been. I now play it to my young children, because although they won't be able to remember when they first heard it, I will.'

I fell in love with the song for the same reason I fell in love with John Barry soundtracks: because it took me away from reality. In the sixties, Barry's film themes positively *swaggered* with purpose, epitomising glamour when glamour wasn't yet a career option, evoking a sophisticated world full of mystery, travel and sex. And I loved them. He did everything on a grand scale, making music both delirious and maudlin, great orchestral sweeps that made you feel as though you were gliding through space, careering down a ravine or driving at speed along an Italian motorway. A bit like Jimmy Webb, really.

It was all about movement, moving through space. Take Van Morrison, someone else who made records that evoked escape: in the same way that Van could, in the words of Liam Neeson, 'take a walk through a meadow and go home and write an album about it', so Jimmy Webb had the ability to conjure up a prairie at will.

'Wichita Lineman' is only sixteen lines long, and yet this dustbowl epic paints a whole life as though it were poetry, and it says as much in three minutes as many authors say in a lifetime. As one friend said, without drama or fuss, Webb captures an entire existence – 'just a man alone on the vast, empty plains, fixing the overhead telephone wires and letting the passage of his life drift through his mind'.

When you listen to 'Wichita Lineman' – in fact, maybe when you just hear it in the background, without actually taking much notice of it – it doesn't appear to be bound by any borders. It is without a horizon, lyrically, musically and metaphorically. The sweeping strings and lonesome words make this story of obsessive love in a flyover state seem as though it somehow floats above the ground, not bound by time, land or permission – just floating in liminal space.

At first you're not sure which bit's the verse and which bit's the chorus. This was an example of Webb's modus operandi at the time, which subverted the very idea of the 'standard' and was a calculated assault on the traditional verse/chorus/bridge structure, a structure which he obviously considered tyrannical. And even though the song was unfinished, it resonated. Bob Dylan said in 1965, 'A song is anything that can walk by itself.' 'Wichita Lineman' is one of those songs, containing a sublime air of desperation.

'What a mood, what a song,' said 10cc's Graham Gouldman. 'Jimmy Webb's simple but oh so effective piece of brilliance.' It is a love song, but there is no moon, and there is no June. There's just a guy on a pole in the middle of nowhere.

As 1968 is often celebrated as the high-water mark of post-World War II cultural insurrection, it might seem perverse to lionise a middle-of-the-road ballad that in some respects harks back to a more innocent era, but Webb's heartbreaking song – rightly acknowledged as one of the most perfectly realised in all pop – is as evergreen now as it was then, and still seems to exist in a world of its own.

And what a world, a world created by two young strangers from dustbowl sharecropper families who travelled west to find fame and fortune in California, and who combined to produce one of America's greatest, most unlikely songs, a Big Country anthem of hope, and of regret . . .

The perfect imperfect song.

1: BECOMING GLEN CAMPBELL

> It seemed like fate was always
> leading me to the right door.

GLEN CAMPBELL

Valentine's Day 1966: like every other member of the Wrecking Crew hit squad who were crammed into Studio A in Gold Star Studios on Santa Monica Boulevard that night, Glen Campbell was starting to sweat. Not sweating because of the job he was about to do – having done hundreds of sessions with the Wrecking Crew he didn't think he would be asked to do anything that night that he hadn't been asked to do before – but because of the heat. He wasn't nervous, simply hot. Even though it was only seven weeks since Christmas – in spite of the Watts riots the previous August, which had resulted in thirty-four deaths, during 1965's festive season LA had been lit up like the Cinderella Castle at Disneyland – the former dental office was so small (twenty by twenty-two feet, with a low ceiling) and there were so many musicians in it, not to mention the excessive amount of instruments requested by the producer (including two pianos, two drum kits, enough percussion to shame a small orchestra, a harpsichord and, for the first time in any studio in LA, an electro-theremin), that it was already more than uncomfortable. There was no air conditioning and, like every session in the studio, everyone seemed to be smoking.

They were there because Gold Star was one of the best studios in the city, boasting the most highly regarded echo chamber not just on the West Coast, but in the whole industry (apparently so good it would sometimes pick up the flushing from the women's rest room), one that had been used extensively by Phil Spector for his Wall of Sound records and which used state-of-the-art audio compressors and engineer-specific microphone preamps. Combining David S. Gold's custom-designed technology with Stan Ross's groundbreaking approach to recording, Gold Star Studios had pioneered techniques that would go on to become commonplace, such as phasing, flanging and automatic double-tracking. Herb Alpert, who made his first six albums at the studio, said that a song could seem 'terrible' but end up sounding extraordinary 'after it went through the mixing board, the echo chamber and the mysterious X-factor that recording at Gold Star always seemed to add'.

It was early evening, and Campbell, like everyone else in the room, was waiting for Brian Wilson to tell them what he wanted them to do. They had been working on this new project on and off for over six months (the other Beach Boys mainly singing on their records rather than playing on them), and they were just about to record 'I Just Wasn't Made for These Times', one of the most elegiac songs from what would become the new Beach Boys album, *Pet Sounds.* With small, deliberate movements, Campbell started fiddling with his machine head as they all waited for Wilson.

The Wrecking Crew weren't just responsible for stoking the star-maker machinery behind the popular song, they were largely responsible for its very success. They were the most sought-after session men (and a few women) in the business, earning over $400 a day each (which, given inflation, would be close to $4,000 today), seven days a week, by playing on some of the biggest hits of the time, with an expertise that completely belied their status. In a town of around forty thousand musicians, the Wrecking Crew (or 'the Clique' or 'the regulars' or 'the first call' group, as they were also known) numbered no more than fifty or sixty, an amorphous gang of studio players who were virtuosos in their respective fields: the Wrecking Crew had deep bench. 'There was one point in the mid-sixties when I was making more money than the president of the United States,' said the legendary Wrecking Crew bassist Carol Kaye. She wasn't the only female session player at the time, but she was easily the most in demand, and consequently the most well known. The other players, mostly men, treated her just the same as they treated each other; the only thing that mattered was your ability to play. They liked to tease her, though. One story sticks in her mind: 'I was doing a Glen Campbell date about 1974 in a Hollywood studio and we were done recording, walking out the door together when an excited fan rushed up to our group looking for "Carol Kaye" in the front part of the studio. Everyone pointed to me and he looked shocked. "But you're a woman!" "Yes," I said. "My ex-husband, my kids, my boyfriend, everyone

thinks I'm a woman!" The guys, including Glen, just roared
. . . they loved this kind of stuff. I think that poor guy was
still shaken as I signed an autograph for him. Probably took
a while to get over that.'

The reason they were called the Wrecking Crew was
because they were wrecking the careers of the generation
of studio players they were replacing, the blue-blazer-and-
chinos guys who did everything by the book, the kind of
players who emptied their ashtrays before they left the
studio.

The Crew sprinkled fairy dust on anything and
everything, although in the case of Brian Wilson, they felt a
little like they were working in a laboratory.* A few blocks
along the boulevard, the Hollywood Forever Cemetery had
just closed for the night; it was home to some of the city's
most celebrated citizens, including a veritable disaster movie
of celebrities (among them Peter Lorre, Rudi Valentino,
Cecil B. DeMille and Bugsy Siegel), yet just as many bold-
face names had been through the tatty doors of Gold Star:
Phil Spector, Eddie Cochran, Bobby Darin, Duane Eddy,

---

* Gold Star was also where Brian Wilson would record his infamous 'Fire'
instrumental for the abortive *Smile* album. At the session, in November
1966, Wilson asked one of the Beach Boys roadies to go to a local toy store
and buy several dozen fire helmets so that everyone in the studio could
wear them during its recording. Wilson also had the studio janitor bring in a
bucket with burning wood so that the studio would be filled with the smell
of smoke. 'I'm going to call this "Mrs. O'Leary's Fire" and I think it might
just scare a whole lot of people,' Wilson said. A few days after the record was
finished, a building across the street from Gold Star burned down and, afraid
his music had tapped into a dark force, Wilson shelved the tracks, as he did
with most of *Smile*.

the Righteous Brothers, Bobby Troup, etc. Along with the likes of Carol Kaye, pianist Leon Russell, guitarist Tommy Tedesco, drummer Hal Blaine, saxophonist Steve Douglas and dozens of other musicians, Glen Campbell had previously played on an extraordinary number of Top 40 songs – everything from 'He's a Rebel' by the Crystals, 'Surf City' by Jan and Dean, 'Mrs Robinson' by Simon & Garfunkel and 'California Dreamin'' by the Mamas & the Papas to 'Strangers in the Night' by Frank Sinatra, 'I'm a Believer' by the Monkees, 'A Taste of Honey' by Herb Alpert, 'These Boots Are Made for Walkin'' by Nancy Sinatra and 'Bang Bang' by Sonny and Cher – a hot streak that, had anyone known who they were, would have made the Wrecking Crew the most famous band in LA. In fact, it would have probably made them the most famous band in the country. The LA studios had a spirit when 'the regulars' were working, especially Gold Star, where, once through the famous yellow door, the team would assemble underneath Studio A's giant round clock to make magic. The band were so prolific, so good at their jobs, that it wasn't unusual for them to complete four finished backing tracks in under three hours.

'Music fans, even ones like myself, who have listened in a lot of depth, don't always have an appreciation for session musicians,' said Elvis Costello, who has worked with hundreds of session musicians over the years, including former Wrecking Crew member Larry Knechtel. 'When you're in a band – and I've been in a band identity for a long time – you tend to assume that session musicians are somehow less connected, because they haven't got the emotional investment or the ongoing journey with the music. But that's clearly not the case because individuals like Paul Simon, being the songwriter, even though he had a singing partner, he would obviously have to hire groups of musicians who he developed a kind of band rapport with, even though it would be dropped and picked up and they would do other intervening work, and they might be working with the Association another week or something that might be more of a regular session job.

'There is a little bit of snobbery between band members and session players. Session players think band members can't play, band members think session players don't have the same kind of commitment, but that's a naive point of view on both situations because you'll find band members who are virtuosi. I've had the fortunate experience to work with a number of people who on the face of it are known as session players, but they've been no less committed to the music, and the fact that they can do it time and time again and focus on the importance of the music means that their love of music is more important than their love of fame or their love of the guy who's hiring them even. They've got nothing really invested in the relationship with the singer so much. Maybe that only comes with time and experience. But you get it initially through the music.'

When Costello was first starting out in England in 1976, he saw himself as somewhat at an angle to the music that was made in Los Angeles, but then, as he says himself, a lot of this attitude was based on ignorance. For instance, he had no idea that a lot of Phil Spector's records were made at Gold Star, assuming they had been made in New York. He didn't believe the session players in LA had the emotional resources to play with invention, something he learned only through working with them, and something he would never forget. For him, it is a privilege to have worked with players who have worked with Hal Blaine and Carol Kaye.

And, indeed, Glen Campbell.

Tonight in Gold Star, though, was all about Brian Wilson. As Campbell sat with his guitar on one of the folding metal chairs, keen to get started again, he could see Wilson fretting over in the corner, on the other side of the glass, mumbling to himself and making everyone else in the booth nervous. It wasn't getting any cooler, either. A few of the players had already stepped out onto the sidewalk, thinking their cigarettes might taste better under the floodlights and banana trees, while watching the racoons and the bobcats rummaging around in the garbage.

Tonight, with his bushy pudding-bowl haircut and denim shirt, Campbell was going to be making history. As the players joked with each other, fiddled with their instruments, tuned up, passed around *Mad* magazine or lit another cigarette, Wilson could be seen behind the double-thick glass of the studio, staring intently at the soundboard. A few minutes after ten, he pressed the intercom and finally addressed them. 'OK, roll tape. From the top, guys.' It would be a tortuous session, with the theremin proving particularly difficult to manage. 'We sat there for hours and hours when [it] came in,' said Campbell. 'It sounded terrible when it first started, but three and a half hours later they had a couple of lines they could work on. Brian knew what he wanted.'

'I Just Wasn't Made for These Times' was almost complete.

Glen Campbell had already played various cameos in the somewhat turbulent career of Brian Wilson, first as a session man, having played guitar on the Beach Boys' songs 'Be True to Your School', 'I Get Around' and 'Dance, Dance, Dance', among many others. Then, in 1964, Wilson found himself crying on a plane, unable to fly, and quit touring with the Beach Boys. 'We were going to Houston to kick-off a tour,' said Wilson. 'I said goodbye to [my girl-friend] Marilyn and boarded the plane. Minutes after we were airborne, I turned to [fellow Beach Boy] Al [Jardine]. Tears were streaming out of my eyes. My face was red. Al asked, "What's wrong?" I said, "I'm going to crack up any minute!" It was impossible. I was already over the edge. I buried my face in a pillow and let myself go, hurtling over the brink of sanity. I cried. I screamed. I pounded my fists in the back of the chair.'

Wilson was replaced on the five-month tour by the golden-haired, honey-voiced Campbell, playing bass and singing falsetto leads, allowing Wilson to indulge himself back in the studio in LA. 'He fit right in,' said Wilson. 'His main forte was that he was a great guitar player, but he was a better singer than all the rest [of the band]. He could sing higher than I could.' This afforded Wilson the opportunity to dig deep, and dig long, which he did by conjuring up first *The Beach Boys Today!*, and then, in 1966, the colossal *Pet Sounds*. 'It was an exciting time, with screaming girls, and good-looking Glen bore the brunt of it, losing a watch and getting his shirt ripped by more than enthusiastic fans,' said fellow Beach Boy Mike Love. 'The only problem was, I didn't know all the words to the songs,' said Campbell. 'They'd be singing "[The Little Old Lady from] Pasadena", and I'd be singing something else. I didn't know what I was saying. But the screams were so loud from the girls, you'd walk on stage and you couldn't hear a thing anyway.'

Almost as a thank you to Campbell, in late 1964 Wilson produced the single 'Guess I'm Dumb' for him, which, recorded just before *Pet Sounds* (the backing track, on which Campbell actually played, was recorded at United Western Recorders during sessions for *The Beach Boys Today!*), is as good as anything on the album, with Campbell singing it in the style of Roy Orbison, and Wilson layering it with surging Bacharach-style strings. Wilson had written it a few years earlier with Russ Titelman, but the track had been turned down by the band, who thought it too strange. Both in terms of its melody – filled with odd little dissonances – and the Wall of Sound production, 'Guess I'm Dumb' presages the kind of Californian dreamscapes that both Wilson and Campbell would be recording on *Pet Sounds* a year later, with songs like 'I Know There's an Answer' or 'You Still Believe in Me', and then 'Good Vibrations' (during the session for which Campbell's inner hillbilly reared its head, when he said, 'Whew, Brian, what were you smoking when you wrote that?'). In recent years the song has become much revered, and is, in the words of former *Melody Maker* editor Richard Williams, 'A carefully wrought song of tortured self-examination set to an imaginative adaptation of the techniques originated by Phil Spector . . .'

Campbell had arrived in Los Angeles in 1960, box fresh from Albuquerque and keen to make his way in the music industry. In the same way that, over a century and a half earlier, manifest destiny drove American pioneers westward – as hordes of speculators, migrants and would-be moguls staked claim to anything and everything before them as they pressed onward to the Pacific Ocean – so, during the late sixties and early seventies, Los Angeles became the geographic holy grail of American rock music. Hemmed in by the sea, the mountains and the desert, California is almost an island, with its own climate, its own flora and fauna and its own culture. Those who make the long journey to the coast always have high hopes of it, and the state has a preternatural ability to meet those expectations. So it was back then. It didn't matter if you were an aspiring singer-songwriter like Joni Mitchell or Neil Young or Glen Campbell, an eager bunch of double-denim guitar players like the Eagles or an old British blues band like Fleetwood Mac looking for rejuvenation, in the culture-rich sixties and seventies, LA, with its welcoming Santa Ana winds, was where you came. It was time for a new generation to yield to Hollywood's shrewd, ebullient pleasures.

'If you tip the world on its side,' said Frank Lloyd Wright, 'everything loose will end up in California.' This, everyone now seems to agree, is how the Golden State turned out the way it did, how it became North America's repository for the eccentric, the esoteric and the extravagant . . . the ambitious and the larger than life. To live in California means to live life in *italics*. Which is why the likes of Glen Campbell (and later Jimmy Webb) were attracted to the state in the first place. For both songwriters and musicians in the mid-sixties, New York was still the traditional port of entry, and yet Los Angeles had the gravitational pull of the dustbowl narrative.

The coast was a celebration of fantasy, a Pacific kingdom of sunshine, sand and surf – a life of abundance, where anything was possible and nothing was real. Even then, hyper-consumerism seemed the métier of Los Angeles, and perhaps Campbell assumed that eventually everything in the city becomes entertainment.

He wanted in.

Even though Campbell had a voice with an unusually wide range – a great story-in-a-song type of voice – initially it was his fingers he was hired for, and once in LA he started making his way as a session man, as a guitarist – an especially versatile one, as it turned out – appearing with the rest of the Wrecking Crew on records by everyone from Phil Spector and Elvis Presley to Johnny Cash and Dean Martin. That's his riff on the Monkees' 'I'm a Believer', his fills on Elvis Presley's 'Viva Las Vegas', his chord work on the Righteous Brothers' 'You've Lost That Lovin' Feelin''.

'The Wrecking Crew could play anything,' said Campbell. 'They could cut with Jan and Dean and then Nat King Cole with the same players. "Mary Mary" by the Monkees and "Dance, Dance, Dance" by the Beach Boys. Barney Kessel and I are on "Wouldn't It Be Nice" and Brian [Wilson] put our guitars directly into the soundboard.' In 1963 alone, Campbell played on 586 sessions. Fellow Wrecking Crew member Leon Russell called Campbell 'the best guitar player I'd heard before or since. Occasionally we'd play with fifty- or sixty-piece orchestras. His deal was he didn't read [music], so they would play it one time for him, and then he had it.' When he was working, Campbell's concentration was like a flame-thrower (in his dependency period, years later, he was apparently just as focused). There's an extraordinary clip you can still find on YouTube of Campbell leading the backing band behind George Morgan on the old *Star Route* TV show in 1963. 'My Window Faces the South', an upbeat song with rockabilly leanings, opens with Campbell chugging through some elementary boogie bars before returning for a solo that owes as much to Chuck Berry as it does to Chet Atkins. In this clip he plays like Jimmy Page or Jeff Beck, shredding, whirling up and down the fretboard as though his hands and fingers are somehow independent and making all these noises without him.

The drummer Hal Blaine, a key member of the Wrecking Crew, said of Campbell: 'He was one of those great guitarists who could hear a part once and he had it down pat. He didn't need to be told twice, he just did it. Arrangers just loved that he could play off-the-wall solos, just the wildest sounds you ever heard.'

In 1964, Campbell featured on what would become Dean Martin's signature hit, 'Everybody Loves Somebody'. The same year, along with the Wrecking Crew's piano player Leon Russell and bassist Larry Knechtel, he would join the house band of the ABC television music series *Shindig!*, which also included James Burton and Delaney Bramlett on guitars and keyboard player Billy Preston. Campbell was such an accomplished player that when he was recording a session, the producer simply wrote 'Glen solo' whenever they wanted him to lend some of his magic. As Kyle Young, the CEO of the Country Music Hall of Fame and Museum, once said, 'Had Glen Campbell "only" played guitar and never voiced a note, he would have spent a lifetime as one of America's most consequential recording musicians.'

Campbell occasionally went out on the road, supporting anyone and everyone, but after a series of early gigs supporting the Doors, where he was heckled mercilessly, he decided he'd rather stick with session work. He didn't like the repetition or the crowds, and wouldn't actually start touring again until the launch of his TV show in the late sixties. Touring with the Beach Boys had been enough for him. After spending much of his adolescence having bottles thrown at him or being hounded off stage for being too young or too pretty, he preferred the relative calm of the recording studio. There was a lot more money in it, too.

'I must have played arenas like the Cow Palace [San Francisco] three or four times. The bill was "Chubby Checker, Sonny and Cher, the Byrds, and Many Others". I was Many Others.'

Invisibility was one of the Wrecking Crew's fortes (no one was meant to know who they were, especially the groups whose records they played on), although Campbell was often recognised by the 'talent' because he had started to get a reputation. He tended not to be starstruck, either. Usually, that is. One of Campbell's more famous gigs was playing guitar on Frank Sinatra's 'Strangers in the Night'. Playing along with the melody, he started to notice how Sinatra emphasised certain words, and how he held back on others. In fact, Campbell was so intrigued by Frank's vocal technique that he couldn't take his eyes off him. 'I tried but failed to contain my awe. I wasn't intimidated, just over-whelmed,' said Campbell. At the end of the session, Sinatra sidled up to the producer of the session, Jimmy Bowen, and said, in his inimitable way, 'Who's the faggot on guitar?'

'Being indirectly summoned by Sinatra was like a soldier being summoned by General George Patton,' said Campbell.

Born in 1936, at a time of high poverty and low optimism, even from a young age Glen Travis Campbell had a sunny, upbeat disposition. The seventh son in a family of eight boys and four girls, he grew up on an electricity-free 120-acre sharecropper farm near Delight, Arkansas, ninety miles south-west of Little Rock. His family didn't just endure poverty, they wore it. 'It was the land of opportunity,' said Campbell, 'if you had a car. We were just one step above the animals.' While the world would eventually see his name glowing in electric letters taller than some of the houses he was raised in, life in Arkansas in the forties was tough. The Campbell family slept four to a bed, and Glen used to say that he never knew what it was like to sleep alone until he was married. Being a tenant farmer, his father worked every hour of daylight, in his bib overalls, felt hat and long-sleeved shirt buttoned firmly at the neck. After a while, the Depression started to swallow him. 'Dad couldn't bear the pressure of not being able to provide the bare necessities for his large family any longer,' Campbell would write in his autobiography. 'So he took a shotgun and headed into the woods. He loaded his weapon and was about to put the barrel in his mouth when he was distracted by a squirrel running down a tree branch. He shot and killed it. Almost instantly, another came down, then another. My dad was crying and shooting his gun, and the family had eight squirrels for supper. His children had been fed for another day, and Dad lived an additional forty years.' As if to emphasise just how humble his family had been, Campbell used to tell a story about how, when he first brought his father to a fancy hotel, Campbell senior swallowed half a small bar of complimentary soap, thinking it was chocolate.

For the young Glen Campbell, country music was a blessed release, listening to it first on a battery-operated console and then a proper electric radio, on which he would devour Hank Williams, Roy Acuff, Ernest Tubb and the other stars beaming out from the Grand Ole Opry in Nashville. He didn't much like getting his hands dirty, or his clothes, come to that, and listening to music was much more fun than being out in the fields all day long. He 'got tired of looking a mule in the butt', as Campbell put it in an interview with the *New York Times* in 1968. While the music played, anything seemed possible. While the music played, he could dream of being somewhere else entirely.

'All I ever did since I can remember was eat, live and breathe singing and playing guitar. I worked at a service station for a week, almost took my hand off, changing a flat tyre. Well, I quit that, because I wanted to play my guitar, and I couldn't do that with smashed fingers.'

On the farm, his father would sit one of his brood on the cultivator, 'Then before you knew it Daddy wasn't sitting up there with us no more. He was over there driving a damn goat or whatever it was! And Mom was like, "You're gonna kill one of 'em kids, they'll fall off of there!"'

When he was four, a $5 three-quarter-size Sears, Roebuck and Co. guitar arrived for Campbell via mail order, sent from his uncle Boo, and his hands immediately took to the strings. He was also blessed with a sweet tenor voice, which he used to sing gospel hymns at church every Sunday; this in itself was remarkable, seeing that he had almost drowned at the age of two (technically speaking, he died for thirty seconds or so, when he became submerged in a local stream after he got his leg trapped in a willow tree), and so had a reduced lung capacity. But it was his dexterity with a guitar that was really impressive. By the age of six, Campbell was performing on local radio, and by his teens he was playing in dive bars in town, showing off his guitar skills, as well as the small tough-guy cartoon dagger on his upper left arm (proudly scratched with a needle and filled with ink at the age of nine). In 1954, aged seventeen, he suddenly quit school ('No point') and moved to Albuquerque, where he started playing guitar in his uncle's band, Dick Bills and the Sandia Mountain Boys, regularly being kicked off the stage of cowpoke bars like the Hitching Post and the Ace of Clubs by the local police, who could see that he was underage.

'They should have had "Fightin' And Dancin' Nightly" advertised outside some of those clubs,' he said. 'I was playing at a place called the Hitching Post, and some of the guys I worked with in the daytime, they would come out and dance. Some cowboy would smart off to them, and they would jump right in. I would take my guitar and hide it. Protect it. If a flying bottle hit it, man, you couldn't replace it. I never thought of shielding myself, the first thing I thought of was, get the guitar out of the way.'

He also appeared on his uncle's radio show and on *K Circle B Time*, the local children's programme on KOB TV. Finally, in 1958, desperate to branch out on his own, he formed his own band, the Western Wranglers, sometimes playing fourteen sets a week.

'There are some good licks in rock and roll stuff, but it's basically one- or two-dimensional, something like that,' said Campbell in 2011. 'When I started playing, I listened to Django Reinhardt. I got a tape – it was him and Stéphane Grappelli. Django Reinhardt was the best guitar player that ever lived on this earth. He would play stuff that was just alien, man. I sat there and just laughed as I listened to his record. And they did all those songs from way back, like "Sheik of Araby". He'd do the lick and then he'd play his own lick over it. I wish he had lived long enough to have recorded some more of those songs, because they would have been wall burners, you know what I mean?

'I listened to it strictly for the music. I wanted to listen to what I wanted to play and sing. I was given the freedom to do that with my uncle and the band. I was a very young kid and they said, "Just play what comes in your head – make up a song if you can." That didn't hold up for very long. I said, "Oh, I love you darlin'" or some dumb thing. It was probably as abstract as that. When I went out to California, that was the whole ball game right there. I got to see some of the best players in the world then. Wow, it was something.'

It was the move to LA that would really prove to be fortuitous, though. 'I'd have to pick cotton for a year to make what I'd make in a week in LA,' he said. He charmed his way into recording sessions, auditioned for record-company executives outside their offices and gradually hustled his way into a living. He played on demos and records, and even started making them himself, singing, playing guitar – anything that they wanted him to. On and on he did this, day in and day out, week in, month out. Happy to play with other people, his ambition had always been to make it on his own as a professional singer.

'I probably had it in the back of my head to be an artist, but I was making so much money doing studio work, I didn't want to go through that routine of going out doing gigs for $100 a night. You could make more than that doing a session. I was hanging around the greatest musicians in the world and that's how you learn how to play. I got to work with so many great people – Nat King Cole, for me that was a thrill, and I'd much rather be doing that than going out and playing some joint.'

Crest Records eventually signed him as a solo artist, and tried to promote him as an instrumentalist, scoring a minor hit in 1961 with an old-fashioned ballad called 'Turn Around, Look at Me' that Campbell had actually written himself. He did a lot of jingle work, too, musically espousing the benefits of various household products, including hairsprays and room deodorisers, while earning enough to buy a nicely appointed four-bedroom home on Satsuma Street in North Hollywood and lease a brand-new gold Cadillac. The covers of his early records featured Campbell in various engaging poses, all of which were semaphoring the duality of his down-home appeal and his 'Look out, world, here I come' ambitions.

Campbell would start to call his talent a trade, a skill he had learned through hard work, practice and an aptitude that he never took for granted. One of the reasons he became so popular at recording sessions was as much to do with his open personality as it was his virtuosity. 'I think I practiced my trade enough, which is singing and playing, being a musician and a singer, to have people recognise that and call me,' he told the journalist Gary James once. 'You know, it's like if they call you to build a house and you don't know how to build a house, you're not going to get the job. I was ready when I was called to do something; I could do it musically. I didn't limit my talent by pursuing one particular kind of music. I didn't limit it by pursuing jazz or pursuing country or pursuing pop. Music was my world before they started putting a label on it. If somebody heard music that was different from another section of the country, they'd label it. That Detroit Sound, you record it in LA, it sounds the same way to me. So people label music. That came from working in my uncle's band in Albuquerque. We had a five day a week radio show, six, seven years. You use up a lot of material doing that. We did everything from country to pop, when rock came along.'

The small success of 'Turn Around, Look at Me' helped Campbell get a record deal with Capitol Records in 1962. His first release for Capitol, a cover of Al Dexter's 1944 number-one country hit 'Too Late to Worry, Too Blue to Cry', provided Campbell with another minor pop entry, but when subsequent singles failed to chart, Capitol strongly considered dropping him from the label. Already into his second marriage – a life on the road was already proving to be somewhat tempting, especially for a good-looking young man – he threw himself into the Hollywood music scene, making home life even more challenging.

In a last-ditch effort, Campbell was teamed with the producer Al De Lory in 1966. They collaborated initially on a song called 'Burning Bridges', which became Campbell's first Top 20 country hit in early 1967. Then came his crossover version of John Hartford's jaunty country song 'Gentle on My Mind'.

And it made him a star.

'I bounced around four or five producers before I said, "But you don't understand that's not what I want to do,"' said Campbell. 'When you go with a company like Capitol, you tend to go along with what they say. No one ever seemed to ask me what I wanted to do. Finally, I worked out an arrangement with Al De Lory where I could do a couple of songs of my own on each session . . . And if he wanted me to cut "Come to Jesus" in A-flat, I'd do it as long as I could get my lick in.'

He had heard Hartford's original one day in the studio, and immediately decided he wanted to try it himself. It's hardly surprising, given that Hartford's version was almost comically country – twangy, in essence – and not the kind of thing that would have troubled the pop charts. The song would go on to win Grammys, but Hartford's version was only a modest success. As soon as he heard it, Campbell scrambled into action, arranging the song in a completely different way, before asking various Wrecking Crew members to play on a demo and leaving it in the studio for De

Lory to find. 'Because I didn't record the song in what I thought would be my final voice, I might, unintentionally, have incorporated a casualness that matched the song's unusual arrangement,' said Campbell, who at the time possessed a faultless five-octave range. Without telling him, De Lory simply tidied up the demo, while Capitol liked the record so much they released it immediately. It was a tactic Campbell would be mindful of.

2: BECOMING JIMMY WEBB

> I remember writing a letter to my
> father that said, 'Dad, you were
> wrong, I'm making money!'

> JIMMY WEBB

In 1961, like most fourteen-year-old boys Jimmy Webb was obsessed with three things: music, cars and girls. In an effort to curb these distractions, his Baptist minister father had arranged a part-time job for his son: working for a local farmer near Laverne, Oklahoma, ploughing wheat fields. One day, while listening to music on the green plastic transistor radio that hung from the tractor's wing mirror, the young Jimmy Webb heard a song called 'Turn Around, Look at Me', sung by a new artist called Glen Campbell.

Webb loved that record, really loved it, not just because of the tune, but mainly for the voice, which he thought was sweet and true. Rather old-fashioned.

'I had just heard the most beautiful record I ever heard in my young life: song, singer and arrangement in perfect balance,' Webb said. So moved was he that he lost control of the tractor, crashing it into the flower beds planted by the farmer's wife. That night, he kneeled by his bedside in his parents' home in Elk City, Oklahoma, and prayed that one day he would write a song half as good as the one he'd heard earlier. Cheekily, he added an extra prayer, asking to have Glen Campbell, the man whom he'd just heard on the radio, record one of his songs. 'The chances of that happening were astronomical, or rather the chances against that happening were astronomical,' said Webb. 'But somehow or another, that prayer was heard.' That day would come in 1967, when Campbell released his version of Webb's song 'By the Time I Get to Phoenix'.

'I'd say there was a profound connection between us very early on that he was not aware of, but I was,' said Webb. 'Because I had heard his first record, that beautiful song, and I'd deliberately set out to create things like that. So perhaps it's not all that strange that, years later, he should run across my songs and sense that they were perfect for him.'

A columnist from the *New Yorker* once accused Webb of writing songs that sounded like hymns, and when Webb was asked if he thought this was true, he said that he would be surprised if it weren't. 'My mother's dream was for me to become a church pianist,' he said. 'My father was a minister, and I used to go with him to evangelical meetings. It was my first look at show business. I don't mean that disrespectfully. I mean it was a performance, and you didn't want to make a mistake.'

Webb was born in 1946 in Elk City, Oklahoma, and raised in Wichita Falls, Texas, where his father was enrolled in J. Frank Norris's Bible Baptist Seminary. Like Glen Campbell, the family business was sharecropping, and Webb's grandfather had been a tenant farmer near the Cimarron River. Oklahoma was Big Country, as was Texas, and Webb suited it well. 'I'm almost claustrophobic,' he said once. 'I start feeling hemmed in very quickly. To me, the ocean strikes the same chord in my mind as the high plains of Oklahoma, which are basically flat. The old timers up there say, "You stand up on this little hill right here. You can see for fifty miles over into New Mexico." Well, it's probably true. You can see a hell of a long way out there. That feeling of boundlessness, I get chills a little bit thinking about it.' Coincidentally, Campbell would often complain about suffering from claustrophobia, too, hating being contained within small places and increasingly thinking about home. Logically, this made no sense, as he needed to go west in order to make his fortune, which was kick-started by hundreds of hours cooped up in tiny recording studios; but towards the end of his career Campbell longed for the Big Country, and his interviews would be full of references to being trapped.

The Webb clan lived in a trailer the size of a rowboat, situated at the end of the runway at Sheppard Air Force Base. 'When the B-36 Peacemakers would rotate and climb reluctantly skyward with all six pusher props and four jets screaming, the noise would rearrange the knives and forks in the flatware drawer. I remember the plane's primeval throb somewhere deep in my chest even though I was only four years old.'

His mother sweated out the hot, humid nights in that sausage can of a trailer, with little Jimmy and his younger sister Janice 'wondering where we were going, what we were doing. But Dad's answer was that God always knew where we were going even if we didn't, and she was enough in love with him to go along.'

Again, like Glen Campbell, Webb was a protégé. He started playing piano when he was six, and for the first few years played exclusively by ear. 'I guess you could say that it was a form of show business, as I'd go on the road with my dad and play piano for him, so that aspect of it, getting out in front of the public, that all came from church,' he said. 'In terms of the lyrics, and what I started writing about, I guess I was heavily influenced by country music, Hank Williams, and all the fine country writers that my dad used to listen to. I couldn't listen to Elvis Presley in my dad's car as he was always listening to country.'

In Elk City, he began playing in rudimentary rock and roll bands, getting together with school friends to dress up, invent doo-wop songs and grease their quiffs. In 1958, when he was twelve, he wrote his first real song, 'Someone Else' (which would eventually be recorded, many decades later, by Art Garfunkel). As a budding songwriter he was influenced by his exposure to hymns in the church, but also by classical music, and of course by the pop on the radio. He tried to emulate the Brill Building songs of Gerry Goffin and Carole King, and Barry Mann and Cynthia Weil. He loved Burt Bacharach and Hal David, the Beach Boys and the work of Teddy Randazzo.

Webb senior was almost pathologically peripatetic, moving the family first to Pampa (bang in the middle of the

Texas Panhandle), Eldorado (not the fabled city of gold but yet another town in Oklahoma), Oklahoma City itself and then the teeniest of small towns, Laverne, a nothing hitching post in Harper County (to find any place in Harper County, you just stopped at the one traffic light and looked in all four directions). For Webb's father, it was almost as though the quest would one day reinforce his belief.

In 1962, the family moved yet again, to San Bernardino, California, in the heart of the Inland Empire, imagining a world of exotic flora, green grass, swimming pools, and acres and acres of palms. As it was, the Webbs' home was somewhat more prosaic, while any ideas of a domestic routine were tragically short-lived. As Webb was graduating from high school, barely two years later, his mother suddenly died, aged only thirty-six, of complications resulting from an inoperable brain tumour. It was, said Webb, 'like a nuclear explosion going off in a very close-knit, very religious family'. As the fallout spread, his father started drinking and then returned to Oklahoma, and Webb, just seventeen, shy and bespectacled, found himself alone in California, devalued and forlorn, with not much ahead of him except a few scrappy tunes he'd written. According to Webb, his father said, 'This songwriting thing is going to break your heart.' When he went back to Oklahoma, he gave Webb $40, saying, 'It's not much, but it's all I have.'

For the budding songwriter, the future was hardly brimming over with possibilities but, inspired by the likes of the Shirelles' 'Baby It's You', 'Baby I Need Your Loving' by the Four Tops, and the Righteous Brothers in particular, he continued writing songs, intent on trying to make a living as a writer. The move to California had focused his mind, not least because he was now in an environment where the shift from nobody to somebody no longer seemed so abstract and fanciful. Plus, the radio was full of artists singing songs that seemed to be stretching the art form, as the likes of Phil Spector and Brian Wilson – the very same people with whom Glen Campbell was currently playing – appeared to be reinventing the art of songwriting every day on AM radio. 'I remember the first time I heard "You've Lost That Lovin' Feelin'", I was driving and had to pull over because I couldn't see. If you can listen to that song and drive at the same time you need to go and buy yourself a heart.'

Left on his own in California, he began to flirt with the idea of taking some of his songs to record companies, just to see if he could do anything with them. He was already enrolled at the San Bernardino Valley College, but at weekends he started driving regularly to LA to pitch his songs to publishers and agents. He had enough rejection letters to paper a wall in his bedroom, but he refused to get the message. He was a professional songwriter by the age of seventeen largely because his songs were the only commodity he had.

Again, like Campbell, Webb had been drawn to LA because it looked like the future, wanting a taste of what had been filtered through to the rest of the country via surfboards and hot rods, David Hockney paintings, the Beach Boys and the Madison Avenue vision of the Californian good life. There was a commonality here, one that Campbell and Webb would eventually share.

Webb was hungry, and ambitious beyond his years. While at college, in an act of supreme precociousness he actually wrote a musical called *Dancing Girl*, which contained his soon-to-be classic song 'Didn't We', an incredibly sophisticated song that expressed emotions the young songwriter had yet to experience himself. (It took him six days and six nights to write it, 'and on the seventh day I rested', although the bulk of the song had been written in a car on the way to Newport Beach to see some of his friends.) Not only was it sophisticated lyrically, 'Didn't We' was sophisticated musically, too – complex, confident, and with a tune so leisurely you could practically shave between the beats (not that the nineteen-year-old boy-man who wrote it had been shaving for very long). The songs he was writing at the time were incredibly intricate, the kind of things very few of his contemporaries were attempting. He was inspired by what he heard on the radio, but his own songs owed as much to Broadway as they did to the hit parade. There was an old-school quality to them, almost as though he were writing for Frank Sinatra or Dean Martin. They weren't your classic pop songs, but they were classic.

He'd follow any lead, return every call. One day in 1965, an ex-Motown acquaintance called him and asked if he wanted an all-expenses-paid trip to Vegas. Apparently, the one-time Motown artist Tony Martin (and husband of Cyd Charisse) was looking for new material and wanted to hear what 'the kid' had. He was appearing at the Riviera Hotel and wanted Webb to come and pitch to him directly.

So Webb flew to Vegas and was escorted to Martin's green room at the Riviera. He sat in this little, badly lit anteroom in his tatty chinos and thick, black-framed glasses, quietly, nervously waiting for Martin to appear. Sometimes Webb took on a gangling aspect, like a bashful young boy not yet comfortable in public, and today he wasn't comfortable. After a while he noticed a figure sitting even more quietly in a corner of the room. The man was Louis Armstrong, sitting in the semi-darkness, playing with the valves on his trumpet. He looked at the young songwriter, noticed the pile of sheet music in his lap and said, 'What you got there? Let me have a look at those.'

Armstrong read the lyrics to 'Didn't We', nodded and said – he had a reputation for being encouraging – 'You keep at it, boy. You're gonna be something.'

It was a very quick encounter, which to Webb still feels like a dream, but it was a huge moment for him. 'I stood there with a warm golden glow suffusing my whole body,' Webb would later say.

He continued trying to pitch his songs, exchanging publishing rights for studio time and playing his tunes for anyone in the industry who would listen. The more urgent our needs, the less discriminating we tend to be about them, and in Webb's case he would work for anyone who was interested. He was lucky that he was only a so-so singer. 'I used to joke around with other songwriters that they had to be very careful and not sing a demo too well. Great singers loved to have a terrible demo that needed their particular brand of refinement.' Finally, he landed a staff job at Jobete, the publishing division of Motown, even though he was still moonlighting as a cleaner at a studio on Melrose Avenue.

Motown was good for him, as it taught him what he needed to know in terms of studio diplomacy, how to make demos and how to arrange a song. He was with them for nine months, and in that time wrote songs for the likes of Billy Eckstine, while the first commercial recording of a Jimmy Webb song was 'My Christmas Tree', an unremarkable song which appeared on the Supremes' 1965 album *Merry Christmas*, and which earned him $400.

'Motown was college for me,' he said.

One day at Jobete, he was asked if he could come up with a song for the TV star Paul Peterson, who had become famous through his appearances on the popular white-bread sitcom *The Donna Reed Show*, and who was now trying to make it as a singer. What Webb came up with was 'By the Time I Get to Phoenix', which, as it was an incredibly sad and complicated song, was anathema to Peterson's clean-cut image. It was considered too odd, and so unsurprisingly his bosses at Motown rejected it. He was told to put a big chorus after each verse, but after half-heartedly toying with the suggestion, Webb gave up. 'I don't believe in writing songs by committee,' he said.

'They didn't like it for Peterson, they didn't like it for anybody. They liked verses and choruses there. Verses and big choruses. And "By the Time I Get to Phoenix" is three verses, very simple, a very direct storyline. The Motown guys said, "Where is the chorus?" And I said, "There isn't going to be a chorus," and we had a pretty lively discussion over that. They ended up cutting it with a couple of different people and not really being happy with it. And when I left the company they said, "You can take this one with you."'

As a songwriter, Webb was an odd fish from the off, and while he had been inspired by mavericks such as Phil Spector and Burt Bacharach, there was something altogether more conflicted about the way in which he wrote his songs. On the one hand he had the ability to write and arrange grandiose orchestral pop (like Spector and Bacharach), while on the other he harboured ambitions of writing great show tunes, the kind that could be performed nightly on Broadway; and on the other – hey, three hands! – he also had the ability to write highly personalised torch songs, many of which wouldn't have sounded out of place on country radio. In a word, Webb was versatile, which is probably one of the reasons he never really clicked at Motown: he wasn't generic enough. To the casual listener or the seasoned professional, it seemed unlikely – and therefore unusual – that the person who wrote 'Up, Up and Away' was also responsible for 'By the Time I Get to Phoenix'. Right from the start, Webb was a particularly singular talent, and not someone whom it was easy to either control or condition.

He had been hired at Motown by a man called Mark Gordon, who also managed the pop-soul harmony group the 5th Dimension. Gordon was in the process of signing them to Soul City, the label owned by Johnny Rivers, who had had several chart hits in the late fifties and early sixties, and who had recently been the hottest singer on the Sunset Strip due to some incendiary performances at Gazzarri's and the Whisky a Go Go. He encouraged Rivers to sign Webb, who brought 'Up, Up and Away', 'By the Time I Get to Phoenix', 'The Worst That Could Happen' and a handful of other potential hits with him from Motown. Rivers paired the 5th Dimension with 'Up, Up and Away', and then suggested 'Phoenix' to a producer who was working with the young Glen Campbell. Webb says there was a lot of discussion about 'Up, Up and Away' before it was given a chance. The naysayers at the record company said it was a Broadway tune and belonged in a musical, not on a radio station. There were too many strings, too much schmaltz. If the record hit, thought Webb, it would change his life for ever, and if it bombed, his life would 'take a random off-ramp into a small town somewhere, where I would burn out in the role of an embittered band director with a plain wife and kids with bad skin'.

Well, it hit, and then his world turned upside down. 'Up, Up and Away' reached no. 7 on the *Billboard* charts, went Top 5 all over the world and would go on to win five Grammys. Suddenly Webb was seen as the salvation of the music industry, and in the space of a few months had gone from being an unknown jobbing songwriter to a highly rated talent. This was extraordinary not just because of how quickly Webb became famous – and if his fame might seem exaggerated from the distance of half a century, the only evidence you need is that on 29 February 1968, at the tenth annual Grammy Awards, eight of the awards were generated by two of his songs – but also because he wasn't a performer. Webb was a songwriter, plain and simple, smack bang in the middle of a decade – and at the centre of an industry – that at the time was increasingly celebrating performers who wrote their own material. Before the Beatles, no one was expected to write their own songs; after they arrived, everyone was meant to write their own songs, as well as perform them (even if, in many cases, various members of the Wrecking Crew were on hand to add polish and virtuosity). Now, suddenly, Webb was properly famous himself, and as he said, 'the pulse of Hollywood was vigorous and rapid and it throbbed through my home'. Overnight he was lauded as the Cole Porter of the sixties and pop music's Mozart. He recalls reading a description of himself as a 'wunderkind' and having to consult a dictionary to discover what it meant. TWA even bought the rights to use 'Up, Up and Away' for a TV commercial for their airline, paying him $25,000 for the privilege – *'T-double-u-A, up, up and away!'* He was not yet twenty-four, and life beyond the age of thirty was unimaginable.

Glen Campbell didn't need to be sold on 'Phoenix' either, as he had already heard Johnny Rivers's version as he was driving to Gold Star Studios one day. Slapping the steering wheel with both hands, with typical confidence he said to himself, '"I could cut that record and make a hit out of it."

I was homesick at the time, and was going back to Phoenix a lot, tracing back my steps to home, so it really resonated.'

Initially Webb wasn't sure that Campbell was the right person to record it, although he was certainly more suitable than either Paul Peterson or Johnny Rivers. 'There was some kind of a surreal fit between his voice and those songs,' said Webb. 'It's very hard for me to look back and say, "Oh, a-ha, now I see why we were successful." Because at the time it certainly wasn't anything that I was in control of.'

'By the Time I Get to Phoenix' is where Campbell and his team first used sweeping strings to offset the confessional nature of Webb's somewhat sombre lyrics, adding some sweetness to the melodrama. Campbell worked on the song with Al De Lory, and between them they altered the arrangement and then layered it with the kind of lush, sophisticated, almost cinematic strings that wouldn't normally have been used on a country song. Between them, almost accidentally, they had created an entirely novel kind of mature pop: countrypolitan.

And it worked. It was maudlin, wistful and structured rather oddly, and yet 'By the Time I Get to Phoenix' was a huge commercial hit for Campbell, reaching no. 2 on *Billboard*'s Hot Country singles chart. It recounts a road trip to Oklahoma, as the narrator imagines what his lover is up to back home when she finds the note he left telling her he's leaving – for good this time. Frank Sinatra would call Jimmy Webb's subtle, almost somnambulant song the best saloon song he'd ever heard (although he also appears to have said the same thing about Webb's 'Didn't We' – 'This torch song is as big as the one on the Statue of Liberty,' he said), but it wasn't written in a traditional linear way, as it didn't appear to have a traditional chorus.

What he delivered was a cross-genre pop-country classic that had both melodic sophistication and lyrical piquancy: a wistful vocal offset by a beautiful melody, and of course a heavily orchestrated arrangement sweetening those bittersweet lyrics. 'Jimmy Webb is just an exceptional writer,' said Campbell. 'He pours his heart out, and the music comes from the heart, the chord progressions running to so many different [directions]. I used to do a lot of hillbilly music when I was a kid, you know you'd get, "Oh darlin' I love you, do you love me no more?" You know, I thought that was good, but then when I started getting into the Jimmy Webb end of everything I was just "wow". It really opened my eyes up.'

'One thing you must admit is that [Phoenix] has a beginning, a middle and an end,' said Webb. 'It tells a story with a certain clarity and pathos. And that would be my description of a songwriter's job. And we don't have much time to do it! We don't have as much time as Norman Mailer had to write *Ancient Evenings*. It used to be two and a half minutes, then three, then after The Righteous Brothers' "You've Lost That Lovin' Feeling" they said we could have a bit more. Then of course Richard [Harris] and I came along and busted that all to hell with "MacArthur Park".'

When Campbell was interviewed by the *New York Times* later in the year, he said, 'A change has come over country music lately. They're not shuckin' it right off the cob any-more. Roger Miller opened a lot of people's eyes to the possibilities of country music, and it's making more impact now because it's earthy material, stories, and things that happen to everyday people. I call it People Music.'

This didn't pass unnoticed. *Rolling Stone*, which unsur-prisingly spent most of its time embroiling itself in the world of alternative culture, immediately saw this for what it was: new. 'It is becoming fashionable in the trade to eschew such terms as pop-country, town and country, and contemporary-country, presumably because no two people agree on what they mean,' wrote the magazine's John Grissim Jr in June 1969. 'A year ago the use of hyphenated hybrids had more validity, if only to distinguish Hollywood's country sound from that of Nashville, at least until Music City caught up. Now both cities have finally got it together: lyrics are a lit-tle more generalized – no "clouded blue haze" but neither are there such lines as "I would send you roses but they cost too much so I'm sending daffodils." Arrangements are plush, make full use of strings, horn, and vocal back-ing and seldom rely solely on standard chord progressions. Percussion is pronounced but rhythmic patterns with a 4/4 or 3/4 structure are often more complex than those favoured in Nashville. The result is a blend of pop and country which has brought down on Hollywood the wrath of country purists and simultaneously made a great deal of money for Jimmy Webb and Glen Campbell. Though primarily a pop writer, [Webb] has almost single-handedly created a kind of suburban country sound.' (One popular with an increasingly urban population.)

Webb himself wasn't just gratified by Campbell's fidelity to his song, he was impressed that he'd somehow managed to reinvent it.

'There are a million reasons why a song does or doesn't become a hit,' said Webb. 'I've given the matter a lot of thought and I think it's almost supernatural. A hit record is almost a small miracle. There are so many elements. Does the singer sound like he should be singing the song? Is it the right song for him? What about the arrangement? Is it overdone? Is it not big enough? What about the players? Was the drummer too heavy-handed that day? Did he have a hangover? What day of the week was it? What was the temperature in the room? Was it too humid and did it affect the instruments so that it came out sounding flat? Did it have the magic to it that translates to sounding good in a car? What makes a record sound good in a car? It's not going to be a hit if it doesn't sound good in a car.'

According to the great lyricist Don Black (who, among hundreds of other songs, wrote the words to 'Thunderball', 'Diamonds Are Forever' and 'On Days Like These'), as far as Webb's 'By the Time I Get to Phoenix' is concerned it's all about the immediacy of the opening line: 'You're there, you get the picture so early on.' Even though its geography was suspect, 'Phoenix', with its carefully delivered slow-release drama, was like a little movie, a travelogue that sat outside every genre of music it was surrounded by. It wasn't really country, it certainly wasn't soul, and it wasn't a real pop song, not having a proper chorus.

Which is just what Jimmy Webb wanted.

'The city I chose, Phoenix, is right on Route 66,' said Webb. 'And it sounded right on the space–time continuum of the singer travelling on the highway, even though it's a little distorted, going from one city to the next.'

When you listen to 'Phoenix', even though the protagonist has walked away from his lover, simply leaving a 'Dear John' letter, you end up siding with him rather than her. And that's as much to do with Campbell as with Webb, because on the record he almost sounds victimised. Campbell credited the fact that he and Webb had grown up within one hundred and fifty miles of each other as one of the reasons why they eventually got along: 'That's what we grew up with – the good songs, the good lyrics, the good big-band stuff. [Webb's] melodies and chord progressions were as good as anything I'd ever heard.'

Webb had written 'By the Time I Get to Phoenix' about an affair he had had with a girl called Susan Horton, whom he had dated when they were students at Colton High School, in San Bernardino. The homecoming queen had run off to Lake Tahoe to work as a cabaret dancer, eventually marrying a schoolteacher, inspiring Webb to write 'The Worst That Could Happen', which would go on to be a hit for the Brooklyn Bridge in 1969. Horton was also the inspiration for Webb's next hit, his most ambitious project yet, the extraordinary 'MacArthur Park', a song he had spent a month finessing while living in the actor Richard Harris's house ('He taught me how to drink,' said Webb). Such was his fame that Webb was now hobnobbing with people whom six months previously he knew only by reputation.

The lyrics to 'MacArthur Park', like the structure of the song itself, were elaborate and melodramatic. Harris sang the song in his rasping talk–sing voice, and when he successfully mastered the line about the cake being left out in the rain, the song clicked. Originally part of a song cycle Webb had originally called *The Cantata*, it was grandiose, almost baroque, but it worked.

Webb has consistently said that people find the lyrics to 'MacArthur Park' infuriating. His critics initially said they were obviously based on a psychedelic trip, but everything in the song is real. Webb would leave his low-rent apartment in Silver Lake, and then walk over to MacArthur Park, in Westlake. There, between Wilshire and 7th Street, he'd wait for Susan Horton to get off from her job nearby selling life insurance. 'I used to eat lunch in the park,' said Webb. 'It was a place you could be away from the dreariness of a really bottom-scale apartment.' And yes, there would be old men playing checkers by the trees. He says he's been asked a thousand times: 'What is the cake left out in the rain?' He says he used to go to the park to eat cake – simple. He obviously saw it as a great metaphor, too.

The producer Bones Howe had commissioned Webb to create a pop song with classical elements, different movements and changing time signatures for his new act, the

Association. He thought they needed a bit of class, and believed Jimmy Webb was the man for the job. 'MacArthur Park', which is actually more of a suite than a song, was everything he wanted, but when Webb presented it to the band, they refused to record it. At the time, Webb had just been commissioned to write some music for an anti-war pageant starring various random, incongruous Hollywood stars, including Richard Harris, Mia Farrow and Edward G. Robinson. After rehearsals he would go for a drink with Harris, drinking pints of Black Velvet – 50 per cent Guinness, 50 per cent champagne. One night after a few, Webb said, 'We ought to make a record.' He'd just seen Harris in the film *Camelot* and decided his voice was good enough to carry one of his songs. A few weeks later, he received a telegram: 'Dear Jimmy Webb. Come to London. Make this record. Love, Richard.'

The songwriter – who had never been to London before, never even been to Europe – got on a plane and moved into Harris's apartment in Belgravia. Over the course of two days, they tore through thirty or forty of Webb's songs, with Webb playing the piano and Harris standing around in a multicoloured kaftan offering his drunken suggestions. 'MacArthur Park' was almost at the bottom of Webb's pile, and by the time they got around to it, both of them were deep into the brandy. Halfway through the song – which at the time was a lot longer – Harris slapped the piano and said, 'Oh, Jimmy Webb. I love that! I'll make a hit out of that, I will.'

And together they did.

Webb recorded the backing track back in Hollywood, with himself on harpsichord, accompanied by a dozen members of the Wrecking Crew. They rehearsed it a couple of times, then played it right through, eventually using the first take and painstakingly adding the orchestra later. When Harris did the vocals at a London studio, he had a large pitcher of Pimm's by the microphone. Webb knew the session was over when the Pimm's was gone. This was maybe why Harris couldn't sing the title correctly. He'd say, 'Jimmy Webb, I've got it!' Then he'd sing, 'MacArthur's Park . . .', adding an unnecessary possessive. As the session progressed, though, Harris grew in confidence. At one point, he said, 'I think the vocals are a little loud. We need more orchestra.' A few months later, when the record was finally released, he was saying, 'Jimmy Webb! The damn orchestra's too loud!'

At first, they felt like the guys who'd created the A-bomb, almost afraid of what they'd done. They had doubts about releasing it as a single, but when radio stations began playing the album track in its entirety, Webb was asked to do a shorter version as a single. He refused, so eventually the record company put out the full seven-minutes-twenty-one-seconds version. George Martin later told him the Beatles rushed into the studio in order to lengthen the fade-out of 'Hey Jude' using a tape loop, trying to close the margin between their song and the seven minutes and twenty-one seconds of 'MacArthur Park'. The song was a surprise hit in both the US and the UK, reaching no. 2 and no. 4 respectively. It even worked as a love letter. Webb always knew that Susan Horton, the girl who inspired the song, would hear it and know what it meant. 'A long time after I had written it, I found out she had moved to Lake Tahoe and become a dancer,' said Webb. 'When I came into some significant money, I hired a Lear jet, flew up there, and said, "I'm not going back without you." We lived together for three years. Then it turned into a soap opera.'

The song was a soap opera itself, a huge wedding cake of a song, less like a pocket symphony and more like a nesting doll. Christopher Hitchens would one day refer to it as 'the horror song'.

Webb and Harris fell out for a while because of a misunderstanding over a car. Apparently, Harris had promised to give Webb his Rolls-Royce Phantom V if 'MacArthur Park' went Top 10 in the US. When the song did exactly that, Harris wouldn't give him the car, but instead wanted to offer him another model. 'He wanted to give me another Rolls-Royce, but I didn't want another Rolls-Royce,' said Webb. 'I wanted his.'*

---

* Anecdotes recording Harris's excessive behaviour are legion. Once, having been on a four-day bender with fellow drinker Richard Burton, he turned up back at his West End apartment, and as soon as his girlfriend opened the door, shouted, 'Why the hell didn't you pay the ransom?' Another time, having collapsed in the Savoy, on being stretchered out of the lobby he lifted his head a couple of inches and said to an elderly couple coming into the hotel, 'It was the fish.'

3: THE HARMONISING OF AMERICA

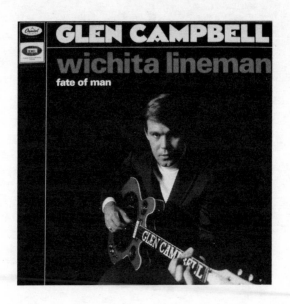

A dribble of bass, searing strings, some tremolo guitar, the drums brushing like tumbleweed across an empty dry highway and one of the most plaintive vocals ever heard on record, Jimmy Webb's paean to the American Midwest describes the longing that a lonely telephone lineman feels for an absent lover whom he imagines he can hear 'singing in the wire' he's working on. Like all great love songs, it's an SOS from the heart; there are even snatches of synthesizer-generated Morse code heard after the lyric, 'And the Wichita lineman / is still on the line . . .'

Although it begins like a redneck work song, 'Wichita Lineman' would prove that Jimmy Webb was a singular talent. Even though he had been a professional songwriter for just two years, he had already developed a discernible style: one foot in Vegas and another in the Valley, composing songs that refused to be framed by genre. Whereas at Motown his quirks quickly became something of a problem, once he was successful they came to define him. Using idiosyncratic structures and anxious, dissatisfied lyrics, he appeared to embrace the Great American Songbook by disrupting it.

'I tend to think of music in a universal [way],' he said. 'From my days playing in church, and talking with Satchmo when I was a teenager I just never drew a line. It was all music to me. I took Jimi Hendrix literally on the subject: "One day there will be a Universal Music and it will bring mankind together. It will end hatred." Because I feel that way and think that way . . . I never closed any doors. I have been open to the Great Spirit to use me however he sees fit and have lived the most marvellous life. I wouldn't trade places with anyone.'

In 'Wichita Lineman' this contrariness would be sweetened by Glen Campbell's calming tenor, a voice that soothed as it beguiled. It was released on 14 August 1968, but there is almost nothing about the record that is representative of that year. Yes, the sonic quality might give it away to some degree, and yes, the lyrics reference an analogue experience that seems almost quaint in an era dominated by the cell phone, but there is nothing here that screams 1968.

Like 1966, over the years 1968 has acquired an almost numinous quality, even though it was a dark time of assassinations and riots and witnessed the resurgence of the right. This knee-jerk response to the cultural, political and sociopolitical upheavals of 1966–7 seemed designed to appeal to a silent majority whose silence was almost imagined as a civic virtue. Even so, it developed in spite of a surge in the counter-culture, which was itself fragmenting into hundreds of alternative lifestyles.

In 1968, San Francisco and New York were the cool cities in the US. LA didn't really come into it. There was a hipster scene in Hollywood and Laurel Canyon, and yet this was mainly a music business/film industry axis, a more gentrified iteration of the rainbow-coloured charm of the Love Generation. Still, to a country boy like Jimmy Webb, who wanted nothing more than to fit in to the glitzy counterculture, it had started to feel like home. Because he was suddenly so rich, Webb's newly acquired abode had become colonised by a bunch of music-biz freeloaders who liked nothing better than sitting by the pool and drinking someone else's expensive wine. America at the time was dividing into two kinds of people: those who lived in a new kind of way and were rejecting the post-war ideals of suburban advancement, and those who were keen to understand this disruption. On the one hand (which by the summer of 1968 would probably have been covered with a henna tattoo) you had a generation who were excited by experimentation and whose lifestyle expectations were increasingly imaginative; and on the other you had those whose ideas about consumption were now being called into question.

Teenage insurrection had been around since the fifties, since Bill Haley and Elvis Presley, although this was the first time that people had started to talk about a generation gap, a vacuum that had started to create many ill-considered commercial propositions. Exhibit A was the 1968 ABC TV series *The Mod Squad*, featuring a trio of undercover cops ('One black, one white, one blonde') who had been recruited to form a task force as an alternative to being incarcerated. The ABC ads for the show were beyond parody: 'The police don't understand the now generation – and the now generation doesn't dig the fuzz. The solution – find some swinging young people who live the beat, get them to work for the cops.' These young people represented suburban culture's fears regarding uppity youths: one was a long-haired rebel evicted from his parents' Beverly Hills home; one was implicated in the Watts riots; and the third was a renegade flower child. All were co-opted by ABC to try and bridge a gap that was only just beginning to form.

America was splitting. When Robert Kennedy was wrestling over whether to run for president, he received letters from irate Democrats telling him to get his hair cut. 'Nobody wants a hippie for President,' said one. Ironically, when he eventually declared his candidacy, he did just that: got a haircut.

To some, Jimmy Webb was seen as a member of the old guard rather than a pupil of the new school, which is why this newly minted LA celebrity had to go out of his way to ingratiate himself with his peers. One day they would all be reclassified as baby boomers, but for the time being they had to battle with the petty bifurcation of their generation. The sixties might be too protean to be hemmed in by calendrical niceties, but in 1968 the counter-culture had really begun to impinge on the mainstream. The Nixon years had yet to start, as the presidential election wouldn't be held until November. That month Richard Nixon would defeat the Democratic nominee, incumbent vice president Hubert Humphrey, ushering in a period of cynicism in mainstream politics that wouldn't truly end until the somewhat anti-climactic win by peanut farmer Jimmy Carter in 1976. Those in the political centre who had been in two minds about Nixon and had thought that his reactionary leanings might be tempered by the possibility of office were soon dis-abused of this fanciful notion when he chose Spiro Agnew as his running mate. While the governor of Maryland had initially been seen as a moderate, by the time he was cho-sen by Nixon he had already swung to the right. Under a Nixon/Agnew administration, the sixties really would be over. There should really have been no doubt about Agnew, as he had shown his true colours by campaigning to ban the Beatles' 'With a Little Help from My Friends' because the Fab Four sang that that was how they 'get high'.

One of the biggest flashpoints of the year was the Democratic Convention, which took place in August, in Chicago, and involved violent clashes between demon-strators and police, producing one of the most polarising showdowns of the decade. Inside the convention hall, Vice President Hubert Humphrey easily beat Senator Eugene McCarthy for the Democratic presidential nom-ination, by 1,761 votes to 601. The delegates chose to adopt Humphrey's platform, which endorsed President Lyndon Johnson's unpopular Vietnam policies, rejecting McCarthy's anti-war stance. Protesters smeared the recep-tion halls with Limburger cheese, which was their way of saying that politics stank. However, what was really focusing the delegates' minds was the carnage being enacted elsewhere in Chicago. Several miles away, thousands of protesters poured out of Grant Park into a miasma of tear gas and truncheons. Ten thousand demonstrators had gathered in the city, only to be met by twenty-three thousand police and National Guardsmen. Some demonstrators were bent on disrupting the convention by whatever means necessary, while others focused on more bizarre tactics, like holding a counter-convention offering the likes of a nude grope-in for peace and prosperity, and workshops on joint-rolling, guerrilla theatre and draft-dodging. For weeks there had been rumours that LSD was going to be poured into the city's drinking water, with some of the more imaginative protesters sending out 'stud teams' to seduce the wives and daughters of the delegates – all designed to unnerve and undermine the Democratic delegates and keep the police guessing. Chicago became a city under siege, with armoured jeeps with barbed wire on their bumpers delivering armed troops to patrol the streets.

Nineteen sixty-eight has been called a hinge point in American history, and as the political turmoil of the decade continued to unfurl – the assassination of Martin Luther King in Memphis was swiftly followed by Robert Kennedy's assassination in Los Angeles during his presidential campaign – so the culture at large started to twist and turn. Traumatic event followed traumatic event as a huge array of social and political trends reached critical mass. The country found itself in a ferocious culture war over so-called values issues – crime, abortion, patriotism, prayer in school, freedom of speech, etc. – all magnified by popular culture and dramatised by an increasingly aggressive news media. It was no wonder that many Americans thought their country was having a nervous breakdown.

The year's most influential song was Steppenwolf's 'Born to Be Wild', soon to be the signature tune of the decade's end in *Easy Rider*. Big books included *The Naked Ape* by Desmond Morris and *Do Androids Dream of Electric Sheep?* by Philip K. Dick, while photographer Eddie Adams helped sway public opinion regarding the Vietnam War when he published his picture of Saigon police chief Nguyễn Ngọc Loan summarily executing handcuffed Viet Cong officer Nguyễn Văn Lém with a pistol shot to the head early in the Tet Offensive. Văn Lém was actually an assassin and the leader of a Viet Cong death squad who had been targeting and killing South Vietnamese National Police officers and their families, but he still became an unwitting poster boy for anti-war protesters. (The phrase 'fog of war' was invented for events like this.) And while *Time* magazine's Man of the Year cover featured the Apollo 8 astronauts (William Anders, Frank Borman and Jim Lovell), the year's most abiding cultural takeaway was the malfunctioning computer in Stanley Kubrick's metaphorical masterpiece, *2001: A Space Odyssey*. Few on either side of the cultural divide would have forgotten where they were when they first saw the movie and heard HAL 9000 stumble his way through his version of 'Daisy Bell (Bicycle Built for Two)'. It didn't matter what branch of the entertainment industry you were in, whatever you did was played out in front of a blinding wall of insurrection and disruption. The civil unrest that took place in Paris in May even led John Lennon to ponder on the nature of revolution. His new song, 'Revolution', was the first to be recorded for 'The White Album', although he was unsure as to which side of the fence he should fall on, hence the ambivalence of the lyrics, where, as far as destruction is concerned, he asks to be counted both out and in. When he re-recorded the song for the B-side of 'Hey Jude', Lennon said we should categorically count him OUT.

While Jimmy Webb certainly had long hair, and voted Democrat, and wore blue jeans, and looked like a sort of entry-level hippie, he wasn't writing about overthrowing The Man, wasn't letting his freak flag fly. His experience was so particular, his success so novel, it's almost worthy of a Hollywood movie: 'A country boy moves to California from his mom and dad's Oklahoma farm and lands a job writing songs for some of the biggest stars in Hollywood. Too wild for the country, but not crazy enough for the city, JIMMY WEBB is lost in paradise. Coming to a theatre near you soon.'

Where did Jimmy Webb fit in to one of the most transformative years of the sixties?

By 1968, Webb was a fully fledged songwriter for hire, and he actually wrote 'Wichita Lineman' to order. 'I'm a muse writer and I write for myself primarily and I write from personal experience and I write about emotional things I'm going through,' he said at the time. 'Sometimes it's political, it can be animal, vegetable or mineral. But sometimes, if you're a professional songwriter, they do approach you and say we need a song about this. And if you're a real songwriter you should be able to do that.'

After the phenomenal success of 'Phoenix', Glen Campbell had asked for a follow-up. Campbell was recording the album that would eventually become *Wichita Lineman*, but midway through the sessions he realised he didn't have enough songs. A few days after the Grammy Awards at the end of February, where he and Webb had accidentally met for the first time, and where Campbell seemed more intrigued by the length of his benefactor's hair than anything else he might have to offer, and after a night of extraordinary celebration for both of them, the singer called Webb at home and asked him for a follow-up to their big hit. He had had such ridiculous success with 'By the Time I Get to Phoenix' that he wanted to repeat the formula and to see if the man who had written it – whom he had never properly met, not yet, not to talk to at length – might be able to weave his magic once again. Because even though Campbell had started out as an orthodox country-pop singer, having worked with the likes of Phil Spector and Brian Wilson and having had such a huge hit with 'Phoenix', he understood the power of transgression.

'Glen called me up and asked if I could write another song about a town,' said Webb. He resisted, thinking he'd done that already. 'And I said, "I'm not sure I want to write a song about a town right now. I think I've overdone that." We sort of negotiated a little bit, as he wanted another town originally, Houston or something like that.

'Then Glen said, "Well, can you do something geographical?" A road song, by any other name. So I spent the rest of the afternoon sweating over "Wichita Lineman".' Sticking to a theme, Webb wondered where his 'Phoenix' protagonist might end up, having left LA. Thinking back to his past, he remembered driving across the Oklahoma and Kansas flatlands and seeing telephone linemen 'hanging against a lonely, desolate landscape', and he knew he had his subject. As a boy, Webb would walk up to the wires, and they actually were singing. And the sound that the wires used to make was a high humming, almost like a drone.

An image occurred to him of a long, flat Kansas country road, with telegraph poles careering away from him in the distance, shimmering in the summer sun. No contrast, just horizon, just a long line of telegraph poles disappearing into the distance and a lonely figure suspended against the endless sky of the badlands. The kind of place where the air hangs like a gauze, where the countryside is full of grain silos and flat brown fields, and where a rooster-tail of dust rises up every time a car clicks down a long, dry highway.

This was the Kansas–Oklahoma border, a place full of solitude, emptiness and vast expanses of not very much at all. (One should never forget that when Dorothy arrives in Oz, she looks around and, awed by all this newfound beauty and splendour, says, 'Toto, I've a feeling we're not in Kansas any more.' And they weren't.)

As cities are so infused with memory, so country – especially Big Country – offers a blank canvas onto which you can paint your own stories. This is what Jimmy Webb did with this song, painting a narrative of existential ennui, a macro-/micro-story of personal longing. The vista he paints sounds like a movie, a cowboy movie, the strings evoking the wide-open spaces of the plains, the harsh shadows just before twilight, the nomadic nature of the people who live, work and wander there. 'Wichita Lineman' in some respects sounds like the theme to a TV western series – if that doesn't come across as being too reductive – a song to stir the heart, trick the mind and evoke the big Midwest landscape within it. And if not a TV theme, then maybe a painting or a movie. Maybe both: an Andrew Wyeth landscape with de Chirico shadows directed by John Ford.

Webb already had a lot of 'prairie gothic' images in his head. 'I was writing about the common man, the blue-collar hero who gets caught up in the tides of war, as in "Galveston", or the guy who's driving back to Oklahoma because he can't afford a plane ticket ["Phoenix"]. So, it was a character that I worked with in my head. And I had seen a lot of panoramas of highways and guys up on telephone wires . . . I didn't want to write another song about a town, but something that would be in the ballpark for Glen.'

He wasn't interested in repetition, wasn't interested in doing an imitation of 'Phoenix', so instead he thought he could do a 'Phoenix 2' and just swing the camera in a different direction to see what it would see. He knew he wanted 'Wichita' to be a character song, knew the protagonist couldn't be rich, aloof or a blow-in. He had to live and breathe Wichita. 'I wanted it to be about an ordinary fellow,' he said. 'Billy Joel came pretty close one time when he said "Wichita Lineman" is "a simple song about an ordinary man thinking extraordinary thoughts". That got to me; it actually brought tears to my eyes. I had never really told anybody how close to the truth that was. He had his thumb right in the nerve there.'

The name of the town was all-important; Webb knew it needed to be evocative and not too corny. When I first became aware of the song, Wichita as an actual place was completely abstract, mythicised to the extent that it could have been anywhere between the Blue Ridge Mountains and the Californian coast, anywhere from Tijuana to Chicago. Seriously, was Wichita even on the map? Because of the song, the town itself now has an obvious romance associated with it, one not entirely of its own making. The name 'Wichita' is derived from the Choctaw word '*Wia chitch*', meaning 'big arbour', a reference to Wichita's large grass lodges, which in pictures look like giant yurts. The original town emerged in the 1860s as a trading post on the Chisholm Trail, which was used after the Civil War to drive cattle overland from ranches in Texas all the way through to Kansas. The portion of the trail originally marked by Jesse Chisholm went from his southern trading post near the Red River to his northern trading post near Kansas City. Wichita then became a destination for cattle drives north from Texas to the railroads, earning it the nickname 'Cowtown'.

In the twenties and thirties, entrepreneurs in the aeronautical business established aircraft manufacturing companies in Wichita, including Beechcraft, Cessna and Stearman Aircraft. The town would soon become a production hub for US aircraft, and so quickly went from being Cowtown to 'The Air Capital of the World', lurching from the old world to the new almost in the time it takes to put up a new billboard. Nowadays it is largely known as the home of Pizza Hut, which was founded there in 1958, and for being the headquarters of Koch Industries, the vast industrial corporation run by two conservative billionaire brothers.

The town is halfway between Oklahoma City and Kansas City (the largest city in the state), and yet it is really in the middle of nothing, a town most notable for a song that somebody haphazardly wrote about it, a town literally on the edge of nowhere. Kansas is cowboy country, a quintessential Midwestern state that epitomises the US heartland, with its rolling wheat fields, prairie, steppe and grassland; a Great Plains state, one of the many that lie west of the Mississippi River and east of the Rockies. It is still regarded as the heartland of America, the backbone of the nation, a flyover state where people are scarce but true; landlocked and flat, the kind of place where the light is almost entirely absorbed by what it strikes. The White Stripes mentioned the town in their most famous song, 'Seven Nation Army', holding it up as a paragon of what they (and those like them) had managed to escape, and what they might one day need to return to (essentially it is Jack White's treatise on the pressures of fame).

At a Jimmy Webb tribute gala in 2003, Billy Joel performed 'Wichita Lineman', addressing the audience as he played. 'Anybody here been to Wichita?' he asked. 'Miles of prairie, endless plains, a couple of telephone poles, and the prairie becomes mind-numbing. I heard this song and it made me think about almost everyone in a different way . . . It starts off, "I am a lineman for the county . . ." and I'm thinking is that a football player, what the hell is a lineman? "And I drive the main road . . ." So why should I care? "Searching in the sun for another overload . . ." Overload, now I'm getting interested. "I hear you singing in the wire / I can hear you through the whine . . ." W-h-i-n-e, OK? "And the Wichita Lineman is still on the line . . ." And then the electronic pulse. Oh, I get it, it's about telephones, and technology and stuff. This guy's a telephone repair guy! And then he starts talking about this voice . . . "And I need you more than want you . . ." I need you more than want you? Isn't that almost like a dis? And then he says, "I want you for all time." Holy shit, he must really need her then. It's as if anybody, anyone you see, a guy working in construction, maybe he's got the soul, the vision of a Thomas Hart Benton, maybe a commercial fisherman, with his heavy gear, has the spirit of a John Steinbeck, and maybe a guy climbing up a telephone pole has the spirit of a Samuel Barber . . .'

And maybe a mailbox out front shaped like a covered wagon.

There was of course no clue as to who this woman was, no steer as to what she must be thinking herself, nothing offered concerning her own hopes and fears. Was she a cheating wife, the waitress he met in a diner, a corrosive temptress or a childhood sweetheart? Unlike 'Phoenix', Webb's object of desire wasn't part of the narrative, she was just the object of desire.

For inspiration, Webb again remembered Susan Horton, the unrequited love he appeared to be able to conjure up at will. He had often written of his first great love: 'Up, Up and Away' was about meeting her, 'MacArthur Park' was about spending a lovely, perfect afternoon together, 'By the Time I Get to Phoenix' was about leaving her and 'The Worst That Could Happen', the no. 3 hit for the Brooklyn Bridge, was about her marrying another man. And so 'Wichita Lineman' became another in a series of love songs aimed at the woman who would eventually marry Linda Ronstadt's cousin, although remain Webb's close friend. 'It's about that first love affair he was in,' Campbell said. 'She just tore him a new rump, boy.'

'I grew up in this flat country in Northwestern Oklahoma where you could literally see fifty miles in front of you, if you can imagine that,' said Webb. 'If you stand on a match-box you can see a hundred miles. It was a featureless world, like being on Mars, except for the telephone wires gracefully draping out towards the horizon. And those wires and the men that worked on them and their equipment was one of the only things to look at. So that was a very vivid image.'

Muscle memory.

'And I can remember one day driving past and having a grown-up thought – because I was just a kid at the time. I saw the guy clearly with a phone in his hand – and I didn't realise they had phones, I thought it was just sparks and tape and pliers. And I saw this guy with the phone in his hand talking to someone in this elevated position – there may even have been elements of the crucifixion involved in this, I'm not sure! – but there he is up this pole talking on this wire that goes for fifty miles and my imagination ran wild. "I wonder who he's talking to and what he's talking about." And because I was a very romantic teenager I thought he must be talking to his girl. So really "Wichita Lineman" is that conversation. It's that conversation without ever saying it's that conversation.'

Although the song is set on the Kansas–Oklahoma border, Webb actually wrote it on a piano in his house in LA. These days Webb says the best way to write a song is to find a quiet place, using a simple tape recorder, a legal pad, a notebook and a full heart, but a quiet place was not what he had when he started writing 'Wichita', as it was written on a green baby grand in the chaotic environment of the former Philippine consulate on Camino Palmero, high up in the Hollywood Hills. It was in a part of Hollywood that was full of chocolate-box Tudor-style castles and faux-Arabian mansions. At the time he said the only things he needed

were a piano, some cushions and some 'good weed'. Webb
was writing for mainstream artists, and yet his songcraft
was of a different vernacular altogether. Rather desperate
to align himself with the counter-culture, he had turned the
twenty-three-room mansion into a living artwork, a house
full of friends, freaks and freeloaders. The mansion was
such a mess it looked like he'd decorated it by setting off a
hand grenade.

'I was living in a kind of communal environment with
twenty-five or thirty of my best friends,' he said. 'My
house looked like a harem.' Guests included Tiny Tim,
Jimi Hendrix and apparently, on one awful occasion, some
serious undesirables. 'People knew you could come there if
you needed something to eat or somewhere to crash. One
day, there was a guy at the door with two women and a pic-
nic basket asking for something to eat. I went down to the
kitchen and someone was making sandwiches for them. I
stuck out my hand and said, "Hi, I'm Jimmy." And he says,
"Hi, I'm Charlie Manson." Wasn't until years later that it
came crashing in on me.'

Four blocks from Grauman's Chinese Theater – in
Webb's words, 'a synoptic garden of silent film's golden
hours' – it was a more than faithful reproduction of a grand
Spanish hacienda. 'It was a lovely big place in a doomed,
authentic Hollywood neighbourhood – a building with a
tiled roof, tiled floors, chandeliers, carved staircases. There
were a couple of clowns who came into my music room and
spray-painted my piano green, I think, because of [the lyrics

to] "MacArthur Park": "All the sweet, green icing flowing down". They thought it was pretty funny.' Consequently, he found himself having to compose the new song while his piano was still wet. He cleared some of the people out of the room, put out some of the joints and shut some doors. And then started doodling on the piano.

'So, I spent the afternoon trying not to brush up against the piano and writing a song at the same time. That whole afternoon was a comedy, with a sticky green piano and several desperate calls from the recording studio.

'It wasn't an important piano, it was a rental but it hadn't dried properly and I was trying to work on it and the piano was sticky and they had gotten some paint on the keys, so I was really sort of struggling with that. It was chaos, as there was a band practicing in the basement, and someone's three-year-old running around, and there were constant deliveries. So I'm sitting there with this piano which is distinctly compromised because it's been vandalised during the night before and I was getting a little bit irritated.'

Glen Campbell would not stop calling.

'I don't want to exaggerate, but they probably called me at least three times while I was working on it and said, "How's it going?", you know?' Webb told me. 'Encouraging me on the phone. Now I look back on it, I presume they were just standing there waiting for me to finish it.

'I kept thinking about the flat country along the Panhandle in Oklahoma, driving along, and I had seen these telephone poles along the road. It was kind of a surreal vista and hypnotic, and if you're not careful, you can, like my dad says, go to sleep and run off in the bar ditch.

'There's a place where the terrain absolutely flattens out. It's almost like you could take a [spirit] level out of your toolkit and put it on the highway, and that bubble would just sit right there on dead centre. It goes on that way for about fifty miles. In the heat of summer, with the heat rising off the road, the telephone poles gradually materialise out of this far, distant perspective and rush towards you.

'I thought, "I wonder if I can write something about that? A blue collar, everyman guy we all see everywhere, working on the railroad or working on the telephone wires or digging holes in the street." I just tried to take an ordinary guy and open him up and say, "Look, there's this great soul and there's this great aching and this great loneliness inside this person, and we're all like that. We all have this capacity for these huge feelings."

'Northern Oklahoma is an area that's real flat and remote – almost surreal in its boundless horizons and infinite distances. I'd seen a lineman up on a telephone pole, talking on the phone. It was such a curiosity to see a human being perched up there.'

Putting himself up on his pole, Webb spent two hours on his green baby grand in his mansion and wrote what he thought was three-quarters of a song. He ploughed on, building the narrative, feeling he was on to something. It swayed. It was morose. It told a story. And he liked it. 'It just wasn't finished,' he said. 'There was a whole section in the middle that I didn't have words for, which eventually became the instrumental part.'

This was the poetry of solitude, a world of humming wires and trucks and trains on their endless journeys across the Plains states. Webb remembered the sound of the wires, looking up and seeing men working up in the sky. He also remembered seeing them from the perspective of sixty miles per hour and spying a little dot on a pole and seeing him come closer and closer until he was gone in an instant. Sometimes the man would be talking on a little telephone. It was a lonely, romantic, prairie gothic image, and Webb tapped into it with a song about a guy who can't get over a woman.

Glen Campbell and his producer Al De Lory kept calling him and asking if he was done, and Webb kept putting them off. He wasn't sure if the song needed a bridge, another chorus or a final verse; he just knew it wasn't ready. Around four o'clock, he was done, although the song wasn't. He felt it lacked something and, try as he might, he couldn't crack it. 'I phoned and told them that it didn't have a third verse, but they were impatient and on a deadline.' So he put the cassette tape in a manila envelope and he sent it over anyway. He said if they liked it, then he'd have a go at finishing it. When he sent the tape over, his note contained a little drawing of a skull and crossbones, with a scribble warning them that the song wasn't finished. Sometimes, when he was sure of a song, when he knew he had written something really good, he would describe himself as like being a hound with the sound. But not this time. He thought what he had done was special, but incomplete. And if they didn't call back and ask him to finish it, then there was no point doing it himself.

Webb met Campbell a few days later, on the set of a commercial for General Motors (a business deal that Webb said kept him in new Corvettes for the next three years), and after the shoot invited him back to the mansion to hear some of his other songs (the GM song that Webb wrote for the ad was called 'Song for the Open Road', and you can still find it on YouTube today, complete with a 'Wichita'-style acoustic-guitar fill). On arrival, Webb took Campbell straight into his music room with the green piano, where they started talking about 'Wichita Lineman'. The composer reiterated that the song wasn't really complete, but then Campbell pulled an acetate out of his holdall and said, 'Well, it is now.'

As he listened, Webb couldn't believe his ears. There was a bright new intro courtesy of Carol Kaye, the sweeping strings gracing the upper registers, and then Campbell's voice, which was more than a match for the melody. When verse three rolled around, he found out what they had done with the missing stanza. 'Glen had detuned a guitar down to a "slack key", Duane Eddy style, and simply played the melody note for note, which was an extreme compliment.'

When they first heard Webb's demo, a few days earlier, neither Campbell nor De Lory could believe their luck. 'When I heard it I cried,' said Campbell. 'It made me cry because I was homesick. Every hair follicle stood up on my body . . . It's just a masterfully written song.'

Webb might not have known it, but Campbell and De Lory were convinced he had written something extraordinary. Later that same day, they started recording the song, in the enormous 2,700-square-foot Studio A in Capital Studios, in North Vine Street, Hollywood; and if the song had only taken two hours to write – incomplete or not – it took even less time to record. The casting couldn't have been better, as the team consisted of the Wrecking Crew's very best players: Carol Kaye, the Crew's most prominent bassist; Jim Gordon, the drummer who had played on the *Pet Sounds* sessions, as well as records by the Union Gap and the Byrds; rhythm guitarist Al Casey, who had played with Carl Perkins, Gene Vincent, Johnny Burnette and Eddie Cochran (and who had also played on 'Up, Up and Away'); plus Campbell himself, the Crew's very best guitarist. (Years later, when Campbell, in his sixties, was touring the UK, a journalist friend of mine wondered why he had only three guitars on stage, compared to the seventeen that a *very famous guitarist* who was also touring Britain at the same time had on his. 'That's simple,' said the *very famous guitarist.* 'He's a much better player than I am, and he doesn't need seventeen guitars.') At the supplementary session a few days later, when they added the orchestra, they were ably abetted by a five-piece horn section, a woodwind player called Richard Hyde, a percussionist called Norm Jeffries and a fourteen-man string section.

Affectionately, the Crew called Campbell 'the hillbilly'. 'Glen was a heck of a guitar player, and I had this Danelectro bass guitar that had special pick-ups and a bridge and strings on it, and got a great gutty sound, and [on "Wichita"] he picked it up and did the solo,' said Kaye. 'He was fantastic, and what a funny guy! He would crack us up all the time. During breaks, Glen would sing us all these dirty country songs or off-colour hillbilly songs to make us laugh, and boy, did he have us going! But what a guitar player. He was great at rock'n'roll soloing. We used to kid him that he was so good that he was going to be a big singing star. And then he becomes a big singing star. I heard "Wichita Lineman" at a drug store one time, and it just brought tears to my eyes, because that tune meant a lot to me.'

Kaye had already become known as the First Lady of Bass, having switched from playing guitar one day in 1963 when the bassist didn't turn up at a session. Her first recording after having switched instruments was 'Help Me Rhonda', and she would go on to play bass on *Pet Sounds*, the Righteous Brothers' 'You've Lost That Lovin' Feeling', 'These Boots Are Made for Walkin'' by Nancy Sinatra, Joe Cocker's 'Feelin' Alright', the Doors' 'Light My Fire', Simon & Garfunkel's 'I Am a Rock' and the majority of Phil Spector's Wall of Sound-era productions, as well as most of the Monkees' records.

After half an hour or so in the studio she started to think that 'Wichita' lacked something at its beginning. A few years previously she had come up with the walking intro for Sonny and Cher's 'The Beat Goes On', immediately giving it a radio-friendly hook. This time she did something similar, creating a jazzy descending six-note nervous-tic

introduction that set up the strings perfectly, bouncily picking out the notes on her six-string bass with her hard plec-
trum on her medium-gauge flat-wound strings. Campbell
loved not just the idea, but the sound of it, too. Kaye's bass
was a Danelectro, a solid-body electric bass (actually made
out of Masonite hardboard) that had a more trebly sound
than most standard Fender-type basses or acoustic double
basses. He liked the sound so much he asked Kaye if he
could borrow the guitar for the middle section that Webb
had been unable to deliver, using it for the guitar solo that
effortlessly follows the melody. 'Jimmy Webb suggested
a couple of bass notes to use, and it all worked out,' said
Kaye. 'I played more towards the end to build excitement
for the end part. At the end, as usual, I gave it more gas
on the long fade, and Jimmy and I went double-time a
bit.' (The Danelectro was also used later by Campbell on
'Galveston', although Kaye tragically lost it one day when
she left it in a car in a parking lot outside Gold Star.)

'The famous bass lick at the start of "Wichita Lineman"?'
said Webb, rhetorically. 'Now, that's an intro. It has a func-
tion. There's a reason for it. On the radio, it lets people
know, oh, it's that one, it's that story that I like, I'm going
to listen. So Motown had all this down. When they cut fifteen Top Ten Supremes records in a row, each one had a
great intro. There was something going on that was valid
and knowledgeable.'

Kaye kept playing her warm jazz motif throughout the
song. 'I was keeping it very simple, because when you first

get the tune rolling, you want to stay in the background as much as possible,' she said. 'Then when he starts singing, the hair kind of stood up on my arms, I thought, "This is deep."'

For her, the session was a good date, just an overall good date that has taken on enormous importance over the years. 'It was amazing to create a nice bass line for it, but everybody makes out that that lick that I played was so good. They asked me to play a lick, so I played a lick. You keep the bass line simple when the tune is especially good and add a few nuances here and there as a framework – you're there to make the singer and not to overshine them.'

The drums on 'Wichita Lineman' are almost incidental, just a brushwork stroll, although the man who played them would live a life larger than he imagined, a life that would outlive 'Wichita Lineman'. Jim Gordon had already played on *Pet Sounds*, 'Good Vibrations' and 'These Boots Are Made for Walking', and would later go on to play with the likes of John Lennon, George Harrison, Traffic, Steely Dan and Frank Zappa. He would also author the instrumental coda of 'Layla' by Derek and the Dominos, which alone would grant him entry into the Rock and Roll Hall of Fame. However, what he would eventually be remembered for is the brutal murder of his mother: having wrestled with mental issues all his life, on 3 June 1983 he attacked his seventy-two-year-old mother, Osa Marie Gordon, with a hammer, before fatally stabbing her with a butcher's knife, claiming a voice had told him to kill her.

Al De Lory's contribution to 'Wichita', however, would be all-important, using an arrangement involving sweeping violins to evoke a vast empty space and the loneliness of the lineman. They were sweet, too, adding something warm and romantic, like snow in a Dutch Golden Age painting, making everything brighter. A few of Kaye's bass improvisations ended up being incorporated into the record's string arrangement. 'Al De Lory later wrote some of the string parts to play the same licks I had improvised on the rhythm track, which was a common procedure in those days,' said Kaye. 'All arrangers did that: Quincy Jones, if he was short on time, would have his usual funky rhythm section – us – do some improvisation and he'd write the band on those licks we'd improvise. An honour, really. So for Al to merely copy a little of what the bass invented for the string lines, this was usual stuff back then. The arrangement was just a chord chart and so I mostly aimed for the roots, or chordal notes, making up the lines. I also made up a pentatonic fill into the chord a few times, a lick that Al De Lory used, writing it for his overdubbed string parts. It sounds arranged, but it wasn't arranged. As many other composer/arrangers do, hiring the rhythm section to create and lay down rhythm tracks, and then copy our lines to insert into horn or string parts – it was common to get the rhythm sections to invent their parts, and using them later in arrangements.'

'Some guys will go off the deep end and start writing for themselves and lose their audience,' said De Lory. 'There is a balance of artistic and commercial appeal, and for me it was always an experience. There is a magic involved in these things, and it is hard to put your finger down on where the magic is coming from. You can't really analyse it. It's more, "C'mon. Let's play, guys." And you play together. As a sideman in the studio, when there was a hit song, you felt the presence of great material. It gave you ideas. You were totally turned on by that song.' At the time, he said that country pop was here to stay. 'It was Glen's voice and the strength of those songs that inspired me to write arrangements that exceeded my expectations.' When Capitol signed Campbell in 1962 and expressed a desire to break out of doing bluegrass instrumentals, De Lory was charged with steering him towards a more appealing country-pop staging post. With 'By the Time I Get to Phoenix' he had come up with a pin-sharp architectural blueprint, and with 'Wichita Lineman' he was halfway through building the cathedral. All those hours working on Phil Spector records had not been wasted.

A finishing touch was to bring Webb's Gulbransen electronic organ into the studio to create the sound effect of a telephone signal travelling along a telegraph wire. Webb had been showing off his vintage Gulbransen church organ to Campbell up in his house in the Hills (during a break in recording while De Lory wrote the orchestral score), suggesting the keyboard's unique 'bubbling' sound echoed what he imagined to be the noise the signals made as they passed through the telephone wires. Campbell agreed – 'I got chill-bumps all over,' he said – and organised for the machine to be dismantled and reassembled at Capital Studios, where Webb came to record his augmentation.

Webb told me: 'Glen said, "Here at the end I want it to sound like that record 'Telstar' by the Tornados," which was a big surf instrumental which had these big electronic effects on it that no doubt came off of an organ, because that's the only place you could find that. I said, "Well, see what happens here," and I just held two notes down, and the organ automatically takes those two notes, either a fourth or a fifth, and it cycles them up and down the keyboard. Of its own volition it does this, and it's a very shivery, icy, almost like outer space kind of sound. It sounded very tech-nological, like top-secret communications or something. Glen went crazy and said, "We have to get that, we gotta put that on the fade." And so he called and got them to send four men to bring it over to the studio.

'We didn't have samplers or synthesizers in those ancient days. I selected a preset that was one of my favourites. I played open fourths and fifths up and down the keyboard with only two fingers, using an F chord. The organ emitted a sound like a satellite or some other high-powered electro device, the open fourths and fifths shivering up and down in a fascinating tintinnabulation loaded with reverb. You can hear it there to this day, sounding a little like the Northern Lights, like vibrating signals from outer space moving upward and downward in fourths and fifths.'

This sound mimicked what a lineman might hear when attaching an earpiece to a telegraph line without equalisation or filtering. What you'd actually hear would be high-frequency tones fading in and out, caused by the accidental rectification of heterodynes (referenced by the lyrics, 'I can hear you through the whine').

'We recorded it, and that's the sound that people associate with that record,' Webb said, 'and it wasn't very much at all, it was just me holding down two notes, which was exhilarating.'

'Jimmy Webb was there, playing the keyboard, and the way that Glen sang it was so great,' said Carol Kaye. 'It's just a good song and when you have a really good song to work with, it makes your job easier. Things pop out real quick. You get the right lines real quick and all that stuff. It was just a nice date, too. You had Jim Gordon on drums. Jim in those days was a very sweet and nice young man. He got that groove on the drums. A lot of people don't know it, but I played the wrong notes! I kept thinking I was going into the B-flat chord, so I'll play a B-flat major seven, which I did, and, at the last minute, I went – whoops! – down to F. So, that's the story of that. But it turned out okay, you know.'

What Webb didn't know was that De Lory's uncle was a lineman near Bakersfield, in Kern County, California. 'So as soon as I heard that opening line,' said De Lory, 'I could visualize my uncle up a pole in the middle of nowhere. I loved the song right away.' With the basic backing track cut in less than ninety minutes – the backing track you hear on the record was done in one take – De Lory took it home to work out his orchestral arrangement, writing an evocative score in which the strings echoed the sighing of the telephone wires. The famous fade-out suggests that our hero has made it back down to terra firma and is now contemplating a long, slow walk into the sunset, strolling like a cowboy, his tools sitting on his belt where his guns might have been.

In a way, the glory of 'Wichita Lineman' blossomed out of an intricate mesh of almost mundane practicalities. The recording process was exactly the same as it always was at the time; however, on this occasion there was genuine alchemy afoot.

Almost immediately, people were trying to work out just why 'Wichita Lineman' worked the way it did. Allen Morrison, writing in *American Songwriter*, thought he had it down. '"Wichita Lineman" can serve as "Exhibit A" in any demonstration for songwriters of the principle of "less is more,"' he said. 'On paper, it's just two verses, each one composed of two rhymed couplets. The record is a three-minute wonder: Intro. First Verse. Staccato telegraph-like musical device. Second verse. No chorus. Guitar solo. Repeat last two lines of second verse ("and I need you more than want you . . ."). Fade. There is no B section, much less a C section.

'Why did such an unlikely song become a standard? There are many reasons, but here's one: the loneliness of that solitary prairie figure is not just present in the lyric, it's built into the musical structure. Although the song is nominally in the key of F, after the tonic chord is stated in the intro it is never heard again in its pure form, with the root in the bass. The melody travels through a series of haunting changes that are considerably more sophisticated than the Top 40 radio norms of that era. The song never does get "home" again to the tonic – not in either verse, nor in the fade-out. This gorgeous musical setting suggests sub-liminally what the lyric suggests poetically: the lonely jour-neyman, who remains suspended atop that telephone pole, against that desolate prairie landscape, yearning for home.'

The song has several melodic skips in it, a technique that Webb borrowed from Burt Bacharach, whose melodies were often unpredictable and veered off in unusual direc-tions. The interruptions and narrative quirks created their own melody, one Webb may not have originally thought of. Linda Ronstadt – for whom he would later write songs – compared the structure of his songs to Brian Wilson's: '[Brian's] remind me of a beautiful horse that will give you the smoothest ride of your life if you know how to ride it. Jimmy, on the other hand, might buck you off at any turn.' His songs are different, she said, while 'the sounds that result from Jimmy's lyrics are pegged to his own vocal style: a choirboy sweetness fortified by a rich har-de-har Oklahoma farm-boy twang. I love his singing.'

Perhaps one of the strangest things about 'Wichita' is the fact that it doesn't have a harmonica on it. When presented with the half-finished demo of the song, the obvious thing for Al De Lory to have done would have been to take the guide melody of the unfinished chorus and replace it with a harmonica, altering the mood of the record while making it substantially more country. Instead, Campbell used a guitar, giving it a big injection of electrified blues and changing the record completely. The mouth harp had become synonymous with the blues, adding a layer of authenticity that a lot of record buyers hadn't been exposed to and giving them an edge that money literally couldn't buy. A harp added instant flavour, which is why country artists adopted it, using it to add vibrancy and a hint of home. Adding some harp to 'Wichita Lineman' would have made it completely western, giving it extra wistfulness and ennui. After all, in a way that's what the harp is there for, adding chills to Bruce Springsteen's blue-collar singalong 'The River', giving some colour to Neil Young's savanna ballad 'Heart of Gold' or topping and tailing Bob Dylan's prairie plea 'I Want You'. ('The harmonica is the world's best-selling musical instrument,' Dylan supposedly said. 'You're welcome.') The harp makes everything authentic.

'Wichita Lineman' didn't need any help with authenticity. It was a huge hit on both sides of the Atlantic, reaching no. 7 in Britain and no. 3 in the US. How strange was that? A mournful ballad without a proper chorus, about a man who spends his day up a telegraph pole. Who on earth would write a song like this? Who on earth would record it? And who on earth would buy such a thing?

'The rule is that nothing ever works out the way you want it to – that's our business,' said Webb, many moons ago. 'But in this particular case, it was a hit. A lady wrote me from Texas and said that she loved the song, that she and her husband Elmer played it almost every day, but they didn't understand why the young man had to die at the end. You have to sit and think about that but the line is, "The Wichita lineman is still on the line." He's still up there, hanging on the line; in other words, his body is still up there. People will take things and run whichever way. But in a way, that's the beauty of the three-minute song, that its appeal can be so broad so as to make it a success with a couple of million people at the same time. How do you actually get a reaction from two million people at the very same moment? That's what a hit is. But I think they're all hearing it slightly different.'

The following year, Campbell and Webb were determined to make lightning strike thrice. Their next collaboration? 'Galveston', another song about a town.

4: THE HEART OF AMERICA

> The Midwest: it's neither
> here nor here.

As Stewart O'Nan says in *Songs for the Missing*, the sins of the Midwest are flatness, emptiness and a necessary acceptance of the familiar. All American characteristics seem more pronounced in the Midwest. Like New York, but then again completely unlike it, the Midwest is a melting pot, the crucible in which pioneers from the Atlantic states and from every country in Europe quickly fused into the generic American identity. To wit: Thomas Edison, Abraham Lincoln, Mark Twain, Walt Disney, Ernest Hemingway, Carl Sandburg, Henry Ford, Harry Truman, Dwight Eisenhower – all of them came from the Midwest. It is the breadbasket of America, the corn belt, the barn belt, the heartland. If the West is the eternal frontier, then the Midwest is the homestead.

When you say 'Midwest' to an American, they see a small town in the middle of fertile farming country. The familiar Midwestern landscape consists of gleaming silos and white houses sitting amidst interminable green fields of corn, linked by endless meandering rivers and hot-to-the-touch highways that lead to rectangular towns dominated by local businesses that line generic Main Streets surrounded by frame homes with wide porches decorated with hanging pots of geraniums and large flapping national flags that all look as though they've just been ironed. Homes suffused with the aroma of coffee and freshly baked bread.

The Midwest is Main Street USA, and in 1968 it was really no different. There is more industry these days, and more fluid migration, but in many respects the Midwest is almost immune to change. Kansas hasn't changed much over the years, either, and it's still the home of the brown dust storm, of tornadoes, of ranch dressing, and – like its neighbours North Dakota, South Dakota and Nebraska – it has a seemingly institutionalised inability to elect a Democratic governor. It is as Republican as the days are long: 83.5 per cent of Beckham County, the largest city of which is the birthplace of Jimmy Webb, Elk City, voted for Donald Trump in 2016. Not only did the Russians attempt to sway the result of the presidential election in Oklahoma, they also attempted to affect their local elections a year later, while there are also suspicions they were involved in the midterms, too. And although Trump may have tacitly accepted Vladimir Putin's denial that Russia meddled in any election, not all of his supporters actually care. One Republican voter who rang American TV network C-Span had no complaints about Moscow allegedly undermining her country's democratic process. 'I'll try not to sound too awful, but I want to thank the Russians for interfering with our election to stop Hillary Clinton from becoming president,' she said.

The terrain here has always been challenging, often brutal, but the Midwesterners' positivity can be summed up by the opening number in Rodgers and Hammerstein's Golden Age musical *Oklahoma!*, 'Oh, What a Beautiful Mornin''. If you were a Midwesterner, you probably understood what it meant to have a Norman Rockwell view of America.

'The Midwest is always patronisingly called that part of America referred to as the flyover states, and as so many pop songs are written about New York or Los Angeles, it's encouraging to hear a song written about a part of the country that's actually the heart of the country,' said the journalist and broadcaster Stuart Maconie. 'The Midwest is always imagined as the Heart of America, that place where good men and women live lives of quiet desperation, and where values are upheld forcibly. "Wichita Lineman" is a celebration of the Everyman, not the small man, not someone forced into submission by the dignity of labour, but the Everyman who stands tall and proud. It espouses traditional values, but not in a Trumpian way, as the song is too nuanced, too odd for that. I can't imagine a guy going into a bar in Wichita tonight and putting this on the jukebox. He'd probably punch in something by Jimmy Buffett, or a more traditional country song. I think the messages in "Wichita Lineman" are too oblique, and actually quite opaque.'

The impression of the Midwesterner as honest, decent and straight-shooting is still difficult to shift. In Michael Ovitz's 2018 autobiography, *Who Is Michael Ovitz?*, the former Hollywood super-agent, and the man who helped invent the Creative Artists Agency (CAA), tells a captivating tale about the negotiations involving David Letterman's proposed move from the NBC network in 1991. As Ovitz scuttled around, trying to secure Letterman a better deal elsewhere, he was contractually forbidden from discussing money. Many would have tried to circumvent the issue, but in Ovitz's words, 'We couldn't address it without running afoul of Dave's contract, and Dave, with his Midwestern ethos, was glad to skirt the subject, anyway.' It still seems the Midwesterner is a romanticised version of Uncle Sam: all the good parts, and none of the bad.

If the American Dream of hard work and upward mobility is alive anywhere, it's in the Midwest, even though over half the nation's population lives within fifty miles of a coast. Culturally there continues to be a defensiveness in the region that probably stems from a feeling of disempowerment, although it's worth remembering that that feeling of disempowerment is somewhat counteracted by the highly disproportional representation that these largely low-population areas have in the US Congress. The Midwest used to be considered the moral heartland of the US, not least because on the East Coast religious belief was rarely associated with sophistication. To belligerent easterners, the open expanses of the Midwest were seen as the places where crops could be raised, timber cut down and minerals extracted. And so the region didn't develop as organically as the rest of the country. While the South developed through its expansion of the slave and plantation economy, and while the West celebrated its independence by being so far away (not to mention by being a beacon of entrepreneurial spirit), the Midwest was tied to the east. It was New England settlers who founded many of the region's cities and towns; it was the East Coast banks that funded the land grabs and the railroads; and it was eastern financiers who invested the money to build the Midwest's agricultural economy, and the manufacturing economy that followed it. So perhaps it's no surprise that people on the coasts accuse Midwesterners of having a collective inferiority complex.

People certainly like to diminish them. Many years ago, in *Granta*, Bill Bryson did about as much as anyone can to indelibly stamp the characteristics of a Midwesterner on the literary passport of the metropolitan elite. But then seeing that he was born in Des Moines, Iowa, he probably had a right to: 'In this he was like most Midwesterners. Directions are very important to them. They have an innate need to be oriented, even in their anecdotes. Any story related by a Midwesterner will wander off at some point into a thicket of interior monologue along the lines of "We were staying at a hotel that was eight blocks northeast of the state capitol building. Come to think of it, it was northwest. And I think it was probably more like nine blocks. And this woman without any clothes on, naked as the day she was born except for a coonskin cap, came running at us from the southwest . . . or was it the southeast?" If there are two Midwesterners present and they both witnessed the incident, you can just about write off the anecdote because they will spend the rest of the afternoon arguing points of the compass and will never get back to the original story. You can always tell a Midwestern couple in Europe because they will be standing on a traffic island in the middle of a busy intersection looking at a wind-blown map and arguing over which way is west. European cities, with their wandering streets and undisciplined alleys, drive Midwesterners practically insane.'

I was staying in New York in the summer of 2018, and I kept bumping into a middle-aged couple in the hotel lift, as they went up and down to smoke in the street. They were from Ohio, and one morning as we were chatting I asked them what they considered to be the centre of the Midwest. And if I got one answer, I got six. Playing up to Bryson's stereotypes, the husband's salvo went something like this: 'Well, of course Ohio is shaped like a heart and so it's always thought of itself as the heart of America, but then Kansas is actually halfway across the country. Michigan maybe. Missouri. Illinois, I suppose. Some would say Nebraska, but then that's more of a Plains state. What about Pennsylvania? No, I would say that's too east.'

When his wife appeared in the lobby with the cigarettes, he asked her the same question. 'Well, I don't know about that. The Midwest is not the West, it's not the South and it's not the North-East. Iowa? Pennsylvania maybe? But no, that's too far east . . .'

In 2017, the Midwestern writer Amanda Arnold said that perhaps what ultimately binds the heartlands together is not so much what really happens within them, but how they are perceived: 'As a land where Midwest Nice is the widespread temperament, evangelism is woven into everyday discourse, where angry people in historic manufacturing cities voted for a racist populist, and where things in general move just a bit more slowly.' She laments the fact that people outside the region have difficulty imagining Midwestern literature – and, therefore, the region in general – beyond Protestant work ethic, American Dream-chasing and the hard-working immigrants of the early twentieth century. And yet many of those ideas continue to define the Midwest, as well as defining the motives for escape or geographical pivot. The *Little House on the Prairie* might be enough for some, but for others their nights are spent dreaming about California.

'Wichita Lineman' is based completely in the Midwest, and it perfectly sums up its location; however, it is just as representative of the West, being full of evocation, searching, hope and a sense of place. It is also a song with no political stripe.

'Perhaps we tend to slight the significance of the Midwest because its history is largely a narrative of the accumulation of ordinary events into large-scale change rather than a story of dramatic turning points,' said the authors of an internal report on the Midwest by Ohio State University. 'It has been a place that encourages people to do what is necessary to accomplish an assigned task; a place that nurtured hundreds of women who in the early 1870s suddenly refused to tolerate the effects of intoxication and marched into saloons and stores demanding that the proprietors not sell alcoholic beverages; a place that produced generals like Ulysses S. Grant, William Tecumseh Sherman, John J. Pershing, and Dwight D. Eisenhower, men who did what was necessary to win wars without being seduced by the charms of fleeting glory.'

Their report contradicts at least one defining aspect of the Midwest, namely that instead of being identified geographically, the region could actually be defined psychologically. Because fundamentally the Midwest is a collection of disparate communities held together more or less by a civic culture that likes to think it transcends (or at least ignores) differences (forgetting for a moment that rather a lot of them actually voted for Trump in 2016).

In 1966, Allen Ginsberg wrote 'Wichita Vortex Sutra', an anti-Vietnam poem, which originated as a voice recording that Ginsberg made with a tape recorder as he travelled in a bus across the Midwest. Ginsberg juxtaposed images of the Kansas landscape with snippets of media reports about the war, linking the violence there with the conservative values of the heartland. He believed that Wichita, where Carrie Nation originally championed the temperance movement, 'began a vortex of hatred that defoliated the Mekong Delta'. He was drawn to Wichita because he was fascinated that so many people he knew had lived there. During the post-war years, Wichita wasn't just a hub of the John Birch Society, it also produced a lot of beat poets, most notably Charles Plymell, Michael McClure and Bruce Conner (along with publisher David Haselwood), who played such important roles in the beat scene that they were called 'the Wichita Group'. A product of East High and Wichita University, they were the first of many young Kansans who would be a part of the new culture that would shape the artistic future of America.

Long, multi-sectioned, snake-like, 'Wichita Vortex Sutra' is an extraordinary piece of work, as powerful and as damning now as it was then (it was used recently in Ang Lee's adaptation of *Billy Lynn's Long Halftime Walk*). As Ginsberg drives to Wichita, his poem attacks the media and the advertising and entertainment industries, creating a barrage of deliberately contradictory words and images.

Vaulting in its ambition and kaleidoscopic in execution, Ginsberg's mantra references a panoply of villains, saboteurs and fellow travellers, scooping up Bob Dylan, William Blake, Junction City, the Viet Cong, the Republican River and the McConnell Air Force Base along the way. By invoking icons of transcendence – Christ, Allah and an assortment of Indian holy men – he tries to reclaim the American language for a greater good. It is full of manipulation and juxtaposition and dozens of scattershot images. 'Wichita Lineman' has only one idea and only a few, albeit powerful, images. Both are obviously haunting in their own right, but while Philip Glass's accompanying music – added to Ginsberg's poem in 1988 – gives 'Vortex' an even greater sense of relevance, it is 'Lineman' that feels the more profound. Listening to 'Vortex', it is easy to think that there was a singular America, one with a common goal, a place where hopes and dreams were shared and where disappointments were kept in check. One day Bruce Springsteen would make a career out of making music that made you feel like making the most out of your life, because it was the only life you were ever going to have; in a way, 'Wichita Lineman' managed to do this in just sixteen lines.

The sound of 'Wichita Lineman' was the sound of ecstatic solitude, but then its hero was the quintessential loner. Who knew what he was thinking? All we knew was how he felt about the woman he loved. He was a working man. He would haul himself up and then string, fix and call those telephone lines in sick. He had a sweat-beaded neck, a mottled denim shirt and a yellow hard hat. In fields of sky-high corn against cornflower-blue skies, he sat way up in the air, way over the horizon, making sure our lines of communication were still open, the great enabler, the benevolent blue-collar Everyman. What a great metaphor that was, and what a great metaphor *he* was, a man who needed a woman more than he actually wanted her, a woman he wanted for all time, a man feeling the need to tell everyone else about his predicament because he couldn't settle the situation himself. Could he keep her? Had he lost her? Indeed, did he even really know her? Here, deep in American Arcadia, was a man in true existential crisis.

David Crary, a real-life lineman who repairs high-voltage power lines across America, was interviewed by the BBC in 2011. He said that he wouldn't change the words of the song for the world. 'I think Jimmy Webb hit the nail on the head. It describes a lot of linemen, what they go through on the road, away from their family. When I hear that song, or when I'm singing it, it brings lots of memories back of storms that I've been on, whether they're ice storms, hurricanes [or] tornadoes. The most important part is getting back to your family in one piece.

'We were on a vacation the first time I heard Glen Campbell's "Wichita Lineman" and I believe we were going to Missouri, about '72, 1973, we was all in a station wagon, me and my two brothers and my mom and dad, travelling some curvy roads. I was the youngest kid so I had the very back with no seat, on a sleeping bag and the radio station, you know, it was a radio station that we probably hadn't listened to because we were so far away from home. We were just scanning the dial trying to find some music and I remember hearing the song and thinking, "It has to be a cool job if you've got a guy singing about it on the radio." The job of a lineman is the person that you see in the bucket trucks that's climbing the poles in the backyard. We work everything from high-voltage lines that feed the cities, come from the power plants, down to a secondary voltage that you use in your house. Sometimes it looks like a kind of war zone when you go in there, especially on hurricanes. This last trip in Chicago it was like a microburst storm collapsing which produces, you know, eighty-five-, ninety-mile-an-hour great winds, there was a lot of broken poles, a lot of trees laying in the lines. We worked five days on that storm, got all these people back on.'

Critic and broadcaster Mark Steyn said that as far as he was aware, 'Wichita Lineman' is the first song about someone who works for a utility company since the pre-electric era. 'There's "The Lamplighter's Serenade" [by Hoagy Carmichael and Paul Francis Webster], which Jimmy Webb's pal Frank Sinatra recorded in 1942 at his very first session as a solo singer, and "The Old Lamplighter" [by Charles Tobias and Nat Simon], which was a big hit for Sammy Kaye a couple of years later. And they're both kinda sorta romantic in that, if there are couples courting in the park, the dear old gentleman sportingly leaves the adjacent lamp-post unlit. And that's charming, but it's not full-strength, searing, aching love on the line like "Wichita Lineman". It's so plaintive and evocative; and if you've ever heard or seen the sonic hum between two telegraph poles when the wind blows, you'll know what a great image of desolation it is – of human connection, and of the man it's bypassing. It's also a very American image – in the sense that in almost every other developed nation the electric lines are buried.'

'It's a working man's song for sure,' said the broadcaster Robert Elms, 'because it's specifically about a man being defined by his job, but you could also say that it's the great American novel squeezed into one three-minute song.'

'One of the reasons the song is so special is because it's about work, it's about the working man,' said Stuart Maconie. 'No one writes about work anymore, they're simply writing about the emotional turmoil of the singer's world. But this is a song about a man with a job, a man who's proud of his job. In the sixties, work, the very idea of work was denigrated, and if you had a job, you worked for The Man. You had to be free. So in that respect "Wichita Lineman" is an anomaly because it's a celebration almost of employment, a celebration of the work ethic. It's an existential song about work.'

This is probably one of the reasons the song took so long to worm its way into the critics' hearts. In many people's eyes it was nothing more than a modern-day version of a cowboy song, with a truck substituting for a horse. Was there any difference between Merle Travis's 'Sixteen Tons' and 'Wichita Lineman'? The fundamental ingredients of a country song were either (a) romantic (and often marital) woes, or (b) job dissatisfaction, whether you were down a mine, out on the prairie or driving a truck. And to the layman, 'Wichita Lineman' was no different. Country celebrates those who give everything they have to their jobs; how the job treats these people in return is another story altogether – or maybe another song. Country songs tend to refine disgruntlement, and there are few things a functioning songwriter likes to do more than write a song about being short-changed by women (or men), politicians, the songs on their car radio, the night, the rich, their dog and maybe even God. Pride permeates many country songs, a belief in diligence and commitment. Loretta Lynn can sing with conviction about being a coal miner's daughter (and Merle Haggard can even pretend to be an Okie from Muskogee), whereas a lot of modern country singers can only sing with conviction about their relationship with their hairdresser. Similarly, on Dolly Parton's exuberant '9 to 5' she goes out of her way to make the best of her situation rather than wallowing in self-pity. Hell, she even hires a horn section in the process.

Working for a living has always been a fundamental part of the country-music sensibility, a genre in which the distance between performer and consumer is negligible. The history of country music is filled with songs about work and workers. The Father of Country Music, Jimmie Rodgers, wrote a dozen songs on the subject, mostly about trains and train men, but also about mule skinners, sailors and farmers. In 1969, a year after 'Wichita Lineman', Merle Haggard famously wrote the country classic 'Workin' Man Blues', which earned him the title of the Poet of the Working Man, although Johnny Paycheck (real name Donald Eugene Lytle) pipped him at the post by making a hit out of David Allan Coe's 'Take This Job and Shove It'.

Nevertheless, 'Wichita Lineman' was, literally, a picture of loneliness, one filled with humanising regret. One critic said that one of the most pertinent things about the record is how desolate it *doesn't* sound. 'It's lush, an odd counterpoint to the laconic lyrics. The triumphant galloping off at the end: why triumphant? Especially when it sounds like he's run out of words? It's a brilliant use of constraint and counterpoint.'

Campbell's voice is emotional, but he's not histrionic, not in the way that Scott Walker, say, or Tom Jones would have been had they been singing it. Campbell's voice, demeanour and tone suited Webb's songs so perfectly because, as the *Guardian*'s Michael Hann wrote, 'He wasn't yet an established part of the MOR firmament, he could still convince as an everyman, and these were very much the songs of an everyman – filled with wistfulness, regret and the truest of all emotions, but the one least frequently expressed in love songs, ambivalence.'*

The relationship between Campbell and Webb was brought up by Paul Weller when I asked him about the song. 'What do I like most about it? It's got a great title for a start, an intriguing title that makes you want to know what the story's about. And it is a great story as well. The third thing is the voice, Glen Campbell. He was a great foil; he was to Jimmy Webb what Dionne Warwick was to Burt Bacharach [another Midwestern boy, born in Kansas City]. It was such a great marriage. I don't really think of "Wichita Lineman" as easy listening, I just think it's a great song.'

Again, it's the yin and the yang.

'Glen's vocal power and technique was the perfect vehicle for these, in a way, very sentimental and romantic songs,' said Webb not so long ago. 'And I think that we made some

---

* There is a strong element of sadness about the song, one that is purposeful and created on purpose. Sadness, or the impression of sadness, is something employed by so many singers, not least David Bowie. When, as a child, he first heard Danny Kaye sing 'Inchworm', he not only marvelled at how sad he sounded, he also decided that he wanted that feel for his own singing voice and to develop the ability to sound sad when he wanted to. Bowie referred to the song constantly, and there is a good case for it being his very own Rosebud.

records that were very nearly perfect. "Wichita Lineman" is a very near perfect pop record.'

The tension between Campbell and Webb was there from the off. 'Well, the first thing he ever said to me,' said Webb, recalling the night at the Grammys in February 1968, just a few days before he wrote 'Wichita Lineman', 'was "When you gonna get a haircut?" And yet I found out very quickly that there was hardly anyone who could stand on the same level as him as a guitarist. And could stand behind me, watch my hands moving on the piano and just play along on the guitar, which is like a virtual impossibility. And partially, because of the tension, I think, between us, out of that came, I think, some of the, maybe some of the nicest records of that period.'

'"Wichita Lineman" works because of the clash between generations and world views,' Jon Savage told me. 'Between conservatives and hippies, between tradition and innovation. If it had just been Glen Campbell, it would have been just straight pop-country, but if it had been just Jimmy Webb, it would have lacked that grounding in mainstream America that gives the song such depth. I think of it rather like Dionne Warwick's "Do You Know the Way to San Jose?": what we teens then might have thought to be Middle of the Road America coming to grips with the realities of the country in 1968. The tension between apparently easy forms and incisive lyrics meant that those two records are more powerful than many blasts of psychedelic alienation. The string arrangement is sublime, and the verse hits an unexpected chord change. "Overload" is definitely not a word you'd expect to hear in a country song. It's a song of empty space and loneliness, but Campbell roots it in the everyday – the character being a telephone repair man is a stroke of genius.'

Rolling Stone said that 'Campbell sings the tune's now-iconic refrain – "The Wichita lineman is still on the line" – in a voice that sweeps skyward during the final moments, almost as though the song is actually being delivered forty feet above ground.'

Campbell's prime strength was his ability to cope with Webb's often ornate lyrics. 'I tried to sing them as straight as I could sing them, and put as much emotion into them as I could. And it really worked. I didn't really care what I sounded like.'

The Morse code at the end of the song was a masterstroke, even if it sounded not dissimilar to the guitar-line intro of the Supremes' 'You Keep Me Hangin' On', which had come out two years earlier. It would crop up again in 1972, as a motif in David Bowie's 'Starman' (achieved through a treated synthesis of guitar and piano). 'The SOS subtly underlines why the song doesn't resolve musically,' said Mark Steyn, 'because, underneath all the stuff about his job, it's a cry for help: the poor lineman is what's really overloaded.'

'People often talk about them as though they're the same thing but our love of "Wichita Lineman" is the perfect illustration of the difference between a song and a record,' said David Hepworth. 'It's a good song, of course, but it's a brilliant record. From the Carol Kaye bass figure that opens it to Al De Lory's strings it's the perfect product of the old studio system. There's just enough ornamentation but not too much. And it's sung not by the author but by a man who sounds as though he might conceivably work with his hands. It's the kind of record they literally don't make any more for lots of reasons. If they did make it now they would ruin it by filling in all the gaps through which it breathes. It also makes me wonder why nobody sings about their job nowadays.'

A writer's relationship with the person who has sung their song to fame can be extraordinarily complex. While someone like Bernie Taupin appears to have always had a completely reasonable and nurturing relationship with Elton John, the relationship between, say, Paul Simon and Art Garfunkel has been fraught, to say the least. It was Simon who wrote the songs and Simon who appeared to object to the acclaim his partner received from simply singing them, occasionally blind to the fact that Garfunkel had a sublime and unimpeachable voice. (When somebody remarked that Jerome Kern had written 'Ol' Man River', the wife of Kern's lyricist Oscar Hammerstein interrupted sharply. 'Indeed not,' she scolded. 'Jerome Kern wrote "dum dum dum-dum". My husband wrote "Ol' Man River".')

I know someone who heard the song before it had been recorded. Doug Flett, a songwriter friend of mine, was visiting a Los Angeles recording studio in the summer of

1968 when a young, Nehru-jacketed Jimmy Webb pushed his head around the door. Would Doug like to hear a demo of 'Wichita Lineman', this new song he'd written? Would he? With his partner Guy Fletcher, Flett would go on to write 'The Fair Is Moving On' and 'Just Pretend' for Elvis Presley, 'Is There Anyone Out There?' for Ray Charles, 'I Can't Tell the Bottom from the Top' for the Hollies and 'Fallen Angel' for Frankie Valli, but at the time had only just started writing. He was on a reconnaissance trip to LA to meet publishers and agents, so an invitation to hear a new song by one of the hottest songwriters in the industry was something of a gift. Quick as a flash, Flett followed Webb into his own studio, where he was afforded the luxury of hearing Webb belting out his demo version of the song, complete with improvised coda. Even though Webb knew it wasn't complete, he seemed proud of it. Maybe he was playing it because he genuinely wanted Flett's opinion, although considering the hierarchy involved, most likely this was just a case of the master giving a masterclass to a novice (even though Flett was actually eleven years older than Webb). Flett was even blown away by Webb's singing, which shows you how in thrall he was. 'It wasn't just the song,' said Flett. 'It was the voice, a beautiful, haunting thing.'

The fundamental reason Flett liked the song so much was one particular line, the dying fall, the line about needing someone more than wanting them. For an aspiring lyricist, this was something else again. And all from the pen of a man who was barely twenty-one.

While it's often disconcerting to be stirred by language that resists comprehension, the ambiguity of a song's words can often be its prime attraction. How many songs that you love, which you can sing along to on a regular basis, contain great swathes of unintelligible phrases, where the vocals appear to almost randomly skirt across the surface of the tune?

There is little ambiguity about the greatest couplet ever written. The punchline – the sucker punch – of 'Wichita Lineman', the line in the song that resonates so much, the line that contains one of the most exquisite romantic couplets in the history of song – 'And I need you more than want you / and I want you for all time' – could be many people's perfect summation of love, although some, including writer Michael Hann, think it's something sadder and perhaps more profound. 'It is need, more than want, that defines the narrator's relationship; if they need their lover more than wanting them, then naturally they will want them for all time. The couplet encompasses the fear that those who have been in relationships do sometimes struggle with: good God, what happens to me if I am left alone?' Hann is certainly right when he says that it's a heart-stopping line, and no matter how many hundreds of times you hear it, no matter what it means to you, it never loses its ability to shock and confound. There is also another more prosaic interpretation of the line, however, one that mirrors Brian Wilson's 'God Only Knows', in which Wilson says that while he may not always love the object of his desire, as long as there are stars above her she never needs to doubt it. Meaning: my love could not be greater, and no matter how much I need you, my love for you is so immense that it matters not one jot. Bob Stanley, the musician and author, says that the line is the most beautiful in the pop canon, 'one that makes me stop whatever I'm doing every single time I hear it'.

'It came out without any effort whatsoever,' Webb told me. 'I don't remember putting any particular concentration behind it, which may be why it flows. When I started seriously performing in my later years, about twenty years ago, I moved east and I played all the big nightclubs in New York, and I think I was exposed to an audience that really appreciated the finer points of songwriting a little bit more than maybe the surfer guys that I grew up with. People would come up to me and say, "How did you write that line?" And I would say, "Excuse me?" And they would say, "How did you write that line, 'I need you more than want you / and I want you for all time'?" I'd say, "I don't know. It felt right, it seemed like a good idea at the time." Then – and I'm being very candid with you – I began to notice it more and more, and then I had guys coming up to me after the show and saying it was the greatest line ever written. I'd laugh. Then it got to a point where a guy would come running up to me and say, "The greatest line ever written!" And I'd say, "Let me guess." It became so pervasive it became like a meme. I have a black T-shirt I sell at my gigs that's kind of a silhouette, kind of an artsy, nice picture of a lineman, and on the back it says, "I need you more than want you and I want you for all time." And these T-shirts sell like hot cakes, they fly off the table.

'I was trying to express the inexpressible, the yearning that goes beyond yearning, that goes into another dimension, when I wrote that line. It was a moment where the language failed me really; there was no way for me to pour this out, except to go into an abstract realm, and that was the line that popped out. I think the fascination comes from the fact that it just pushes the language a little bit beyond what it was really meant to express, because it could be deemed perfectly nonsensical – "I need you more than want you / and I want you for all time." I mean, those are all abstract concepts, all jammed up together there. But that's because it's trying to express the inexpressible.

'I don't judge, but I evaluate a person's sensitivity by their ability to respond to poetry. Not just my lyrics and not just James Taylor's lyrics and not just Joni Mitchell's lyrics . . . because when Joni Mitchell wrote 'A Case of You', she broke my heart, it was like someone swung a sledgehammer against a teapot. I still can't say that line without losing control of my emotions. That was also a case where she was trying to express the inexpressible, so she had to push the language.

'It's almost childishly simple, but it suddenly dawned on me that I was a conduit for all kinds of emotions that people were either incapable of expressing or unwilling to express. The song became the real e-mail – emotional mail. The songwriter is almost a trader in feelings. I realised somewhat later that I deal almost exclusively in the emotional wreckage of life. It's where I live, and that can be really, really dangerous.'

And Glen Campbell, who spent much of his life on the road? '*I want you for all time* – I always say that to my wife, because it cheers her up,' he once said. 'We got some grown kids and they say, "Oh, you guys. You guys are like lovebirds."'

'Good songwriting is still important,' said Webb. 'It is a continuing miracle that an art form so potent and influential in the emotional lives of human beings is available to virtually anyone who wants to enjoy it. There's a subtext to classic hit songs, and that subtext is the common experience. By its very nature, it isn't very easy to explain the intangible hook that fastens on to everyone.'

'Wichita Lineman' sounds as good to me now as it did when I first heard it fifty years ago. It has never palled or suffered through overexposure. I never wince when I hear it. Some neuroscientists believe that our brains go through two stages when we listen to a piece of music that we like: the caudate nucleus in the brain anticipates the build-up of our favourite part of the song as we listen, while the nucleus accumbens is triggered by the peak, thus causing the release of endorphins. Accordingly, they believe that the more we get to know a piece of music, the less fired up our brains will be in anticipating this peak. This thesis starts to evaporate further when you consider that received wisdom says that the more complex a song is, the more it will endure. 'Wichita Lineman' is anything but complex. It might have an unusual structure, and the lyrics might be particular, but it's not exactly 'Bohemian Rhapsody', not exactly comparable to the type of intricate prog rock made by the likes of Yes, Camel or Emerson, Lake and Palmer.

I once read about a professor who ran a music-therapist programme at a New York university. He said we hang on to songs because they are part of our 'identity construction', and that we are always trying to use them to get back to our lost paradise. What I certainly know is that I don't tire of 'Wichita Lineman' for the same reason I don't tire of listening to the Beatles' 'Hey Jude', Brian Protheroe's 'Pinball' or Nick Drake's 'One of These Things First' – because it defies the injustice of repetition.

5: THE LINEMAN'S AFTERLIFE

> I believe that all roads lead to the
> same place, and that is wherever
> all roads lead to.

WILLIE NELSON

There are hundreds of versions of 'By the Time I Get to Phoenix', possibly even thousands, and it has become as much of a classic as 'My Way', 'Yesterday' or 'Hallelujah'. One of the most disturbing cover versions is by Nick Cave and the Bad Seeds, which John Peel once said was the best interpretation, by some considerable distance. The most elaborate version, however, is by Isaac Hayes, who turned the song into something of a Brobdingnagian epic. By deliberately fusing soap opera and ghetto chic, in the late sixties and early seventies Hayes created his own highly rhythmic, symphonic environment, and in this way was as influential as Sly Stone. Both men moved away from R&B and into traditionally white areas: Stone into rock, Hayes into the orchestral world of Burt Bacharach, Carole King and Jimmy Webb.

Of course, one wonders why. Cover versions are often redundant, and rarely remembered. Some can be little more than cheap photocopies, with someone hitherto unknown (or, maybe, far too well known) colouring in the original and trying not to go outside the lines. Some can be transformative, but often they are nothing but corruptions of your favourite memories (I would imagine if you had formative experiences with, or fond memories of, New Order's 'True Faith', you would probably think George Michael's cover is pointless; ditto Robbie Williams's live version of Blur's 'Song 2' or Simple Minds' frankly confusing version of Prince's 'Sign o' the Times'). Others are just plain perverse: does anyone really want to hear William Shatner cover Pulp's 'Common People'?

Another son of a sharecropper (this time from Memphis), Isaac Hayes joined Stax Records in 1964, aged twenty-two, eventually writing, arranging and producing dozens of hits for Sam & Dave, Carla Thomas and Johnnie Taylor ('Hold On, I'm Coming', 'Soul Man', 'B-A-B-Y', etc.). It was his 1969 solo LP *Hot Buttered Soul*, though, which really brought him personal acclaim, and at the time it was cited as the most important black album since James Brown's *Live at the Apollo*, seven years earlier. *Hot* included an eighteen-minute version of 'By the Time I Get to Phoenix' and an elaborate reworking of Bacharach's 'Walk On By', Hayes draping white-bread orchestral arrangements around his seemingly interminable monologues, almost as though he was experimenting with various convoluted seduction techniques. With his lush raps and funereal beats, Hayes gave you the impression he could turn a thirty-second hairspray commercial into a three-hour symphony, complete with several different movements and at least a dozen costume changes. He had a dark-brown crooner's voice which perfectly suited this type of rich ballad, and all the others which came in its wake: 'It's Too Late', 'Windows of the World', 'The Look of Love', 'Ain't No Sunshine', etc. He was a remarkable arranger, and the bulk of his 1971 LP *Shaft* – in which he reached critical mass while winning two Grammys and an Oscar – is almost worthy of Bernard Herrmann. Talking about *Hot Buttered Soul*, he once said, 'Like rock groups, I always wanted to present songs as dramas. It was something white artists did so well, but black folks hadn't got into it. Which was why I picked those, if you like, white songs for that set, because they have the dramatic content.'

Hayes's version of 'Phoenix' is monumental, containing an audacious ten-minute rap that invents a back story around Jimmy Webb's Phoenix couple. 'The rap came out of the necessity to communicate. There's a local club in Memphis, primarily black, called the Tiki Club. One night there I heard "Phoenix" and I thought, "Wow, this song is great, this man must really love this woman." I ran down to the studio the next day and told them about the song, and they said, "Yeah, yeah." They didn't feel what I felt, I thought maybe they weren't getting it. The Bar-Kays were playing the Tiki Club a few days later, so I told them to learn the song and that I would sit in. I told them to keep cycling the first chord, and I started talking, just telling the story about what could have happened to cause this man to leave. Halfway through the song, conversations started to subside, and by the time I finished the song, there wasn't a dry eye in the house.'

As for the record, he said, 'To preserve the vibe we cut it live, with no retakes – if you listen hard on the CD you can hear how my vocal mike picked up my fingernails clicking on the organ keys as I played those big swirls. When I played the whole album back to the company bigwigs they sat there in shock. I got worried and said, "Well?" After a while the promotions manager said, "That motherfucker is awesome. Won't nobody give it airplay, but that ain't even gonna matter."' He was right, as within three months the album had outsold every LP the company had on release, reaching the top of the soul, jazz and pop charts. By the end of 1970, the album was platinum.

Jimmy Webb loved it. 'The whole talking blues thing at the beginning was like a novel – a major opus. It was to do with the Delta blues tradition, that way of telling a story, although people sometimes forget he did a great job at singing the song too. I'd produced the Supremes, I understood R'n'B and soul artists, so it wasn't so far-fetched to me. Isaac was a precursor to rap and hip-hop, he was trying to create something new.'

I remember playing Hayes's widescreen epic in 1977, when the Summer of Hate (©) was officially in full flow, and at a time when even owning a copy of a Who album was suspicious. Back then, owning an Isaac Hayes album was considered contrary rather than damaging to one's street cred. Over time, liking an unlikely or perennially unfashionable record ceased being socially unacceptable, becoming instead a Guilty Pleasure (©). As it was for many of my generation,

1977 was something of a benchmark. That year, I spent most of the summer bouncing between the Roxy, the Marquee, the Red Cow and the 100 Club, watching the likes of the Clash, the Jam, the Damned, and Adam and the Ants. This was also the summer when I moved up to London, at the age of seventeen, to join a foundation course at Chelsea School of Art. Every day I would walk to college along the King's Road, and every night I would wander off into Soho, taking the number 11, 22 or 19 bus, destined to end up in a basement listening to extremely loud punk music.

It was, and remains, like it was for many of the others who spent their formative years listening to three-chord leather-jacket rock, one of the happiest times of my life. At the time, I looked like Johnny Ramone (shaggy pudding-bowl haircut, black plastic jacket, drainpipe jeans and dirty white plimsolls) and hadn't a care in the world. But while it is assumed that when us baby punks made our way back to our homes (in my case, the Ralph West Halls of Residence on Albert Bridge Road, which serviced all the central London art schools) we hastily put imported dub or hardcore industrial albums on our turntables, many of us listened to the music we were now being encouraged by the music press to unceremoniously dump. So while we would certainly listen to *Two Sevens Clash* by Culture, *Horses* by Patti Smith, *Autobahn* by Kraftwerk and various Throbbing Gristle bootlegs (horrible then, and horrible now), we would still wind down (what chilling out was called back in the day) by listening to Joni Mitchell, Neil Young, Isaac Hayes, John

Martyn or one of the seminal records of 1977 – released in August that year – Steely Dan's majestic *Aja*. For while we spent our evenings jumping up and down in sweaty West End venues, we were still dreaming of driving down Sunset Boulevard in a big fancy car listening to super-slick West Coast music. And although the snarky, sarcastic Steely Dan obviously hated anything to do with West Coast culture, they actually made the slickest West Coast music of all. My room may have been covered with Sex Pistols posters, but my heart was elsewhere: in California, the deserts of Arizona, the west coast of Ireland . . . Notting Hill in the late fifties. On the perimeter of sleep, I would lie there and imagine myself living the lives in those songs, believing my own life to be full of the same possibilities.

Another record that got heavy rotation in my room at Ralph West (although admittedly after most people had sloped off to their own) was *Glen Campbell's Greatest Hits*, a Capitol album with a tightly cropped photograph of Glen's head on the cover, poking out of an especially loud orange shirt (an orange that was almost identical to Campbell's skin tone). As I was studying typography as part of my course, I knew the cover type was Stencil Bold, an especially cheap font that gave the whole thing a patina of naff. At the time, it was, I suppose, a Guilty Pleasure, not that I've ever really believed in them.

'Wichita Lineman' was never a Guilty Pleasure, though, never had a hint of embarrassment about it. Sure, it was draped in melancholy, and there were vaporous traces of country all over it, but there was nothing boilerplate about it. Designed to be cinematic, writ wide in CinemaScope, it was predetermined to evoke the never-ending plains of the Midwest, something too grand to be cute. Through the fields of wheat and milo and Sudangrass and flax and alfalfa came the strains of a record destined to define itself like no other, a record with a big sky, a horizon and a man attending to a telegraph pole.

You'll read stats that will tell you that 'By the Time I Get to Phoenix' is the third most recorded song of all time, and although 'Wichita Lineman' can't match that, its interpreters have certainly been more idiosyncratic, and over the years, as the song has developed momentum, it has attracted more and more admirers, and more who have wanted to conquer it: (*deep breath*) R.E.M., Stone Temple Pilots, Patti Smith, Keith Urban, Dwight Yoakam, Billy Joel, Melissa Etheridge, the Dells, José Feliciano, James Taylor, Dennis Brown, Maria McKee, Ray Charles (who gets bonus points for his spoken-word ad-lib near the end – 'That's me, baby!'), the jazz pianist Alan Pasqua, O. C. Smith, Ken Berry, the Lettermen, the Fatback Band, Tom Jones, the Scud Mountain Boys, Peter Nero, Sérgio Mendes and Brasil '66, Cassandra Wilson, Gomez, Smokey Robinson and the Miracles, Celtic Thunder, Johnny Cash, the Meters, the White Stripes, Villagers, 'Tennessee' Ernie Ford, Urge Overkill and more.

Sammy Davis Jr recorded an extraordinary version on his 1970 Motown album *Something for Everyone*. Davis was a great dancer, a great mimic, a great comedian and a great singer, but what he really was, was a great performer. And while some marvelled at his range (one critic said his voice always sounded too epic for such a small body), listening to his voice today his emotions sound premeditated. Frank Sinatra and Tony Bennett sang from their core, whereas Davis was essentially a song-and-dance man at heart, so his singing was textbook rather than heartfelt. But what a textbook. His version of 'Wichita' is almost comically funky, and yet it works. Employing the tropes of the rhinestone ghetto, when he sang it on his TV show *Sammy & Company* he was wearing a coffee-and-cream gingham jacket, a bright-pink shirt with an aircraft carrier collar, buckets of jewellery and an overgrown pencil moustache.

'Listen, I've had the good fortune of working for the past decade and a half or so,' he says to the audience, teasingly. 'And every once in a while, when you have groovy friends and a groovy audience, you get to do something you didn't like to do. Now, those of you who have seen some of *Sammy & Company* have occasionally said to me, "You obviously dig country and western." And I don't want to say anything real strange, you know, but shucks almighty' – his voice going all country – 'I've been known to be called Pea-Picker every once in a while . . . And we do do a couple of toe-tappers. So, we're gonna do a little country and western for you. Well, let me put it this way, this is about as country and western as I'm gonna get . . . I am a lineman for the county . . .'

The most unusual version is by the Dick Slessig Combo, a band who appear to create dreamy instrumental arrangements of songs from the late sixties and early seventies, and who stretched the song from three minutes to forty-three. This is the longest version of any song you've ever heard, elongated, expanded and slowed down so that it sounds even more like a lament, with a hyphen of silence between each note. The first time I heard it, it sounded like Chris Isaak performing an especially lazy version of the Velvet Underground's 'Sunday Morning', before veering off into the fringes of prog and ending up like something the Durutti Column might have recorded for their famous sandpaper album (or, as one reviewer said, a hybrid of Steve Reich, bluegrass and Jackie-O Motherfucker, or an American backwoods version of Neu! in 'motorik' mode). This prolonged version 'exposes just how good the song's "bones" are', said Mark Sullivan from sitdownlistenup.com. 'Yes, portions of the song repeat, but this is far from jazz interpretation. These repeated phrases are not variations, but more like playing a particularly interesting part of a song over and over to properly appreciate it before moving on to the next part of the song, similar to rewinding a cool scene in a movie before moving on. Or maybe the closed loop just evokes a stuck record. Like film, music is a temporal medium. Although spending more time with a painting or a sculpture often leads to a much deeper relationship with the work as additional detail is absorbed, the detail was all there the whole time. A piece of music, on the other hand, is realized over time, doling out its details in increments. Slowing down a tune forces us to focus more on the moments as they come together. Dick Slessig Combo's diffuse rendering of "Wichita Lineman" makes us more mindful of each individual note, but enough of the melody drifts in and out that we never entirely lose track of the whole of which the notes are a part.'

When the song eventually finishes you feel as though you've just stepped out of a cinema during the day, into a sudden shock of sunshine.

In Cassandra Wilson's version, from 2002, she slows the song down to nearly six minutes, and her vocals don't start until she's half a minute into it. She changes the lyrics, too, turning it into a piece of badly realised journalese, singing a love song to her own Wichita lineman and telling him that she needs him more than she wants him.

The song has been honoured in other ways, too. Homer sang snippets of 'Wichita' on *The Simpsons*, the Boo Radleys recorded a song called 'Jimmy Webb Is God', and in 2000 Mark Bowen and Dick Green launched an independent record label called Wichita Recordings (strapline: 'Still on the line'), whose acts included Bloc Party, the Cribs, Clap Your Hands Say Yeah, Bright Eyes, My Morning Jacket, and Peter, Bjorn and John. They took its name from 'Lineman' simply because it is, they believe, the greatest song ever written, while their logo – a telegraph pole against the sky – was the result of a Dick Green doodle in a bar. It's even been adopted on the football terraces – 'I am a lineman for Notts County,' for instance.

The song makes a cameo in DBC Pierre's Booker Prize-winning Texan black comedy *Vernon God Little* (once described as *Huckleberry Finn* for the Eminem generation, the eponymous hero a 'Holden Caulfield on amphetamines'), which uses Glen Campbell's biggest hits instead of a Greek chorus, Pierre peppering the novel with mordant soundtrack choices in much the same way as Bret Easton Ellis does in *American Psycho*, only this time as power lines and fence posts shoot past on the side of the road. 'Instead of trying to figure it out, I call some Glen Campbell to mind, to help me lope along, crusty and lonesome, older than my years,' says our protagonist. '"Wichita Lineman" is the song I call up, not "Galveston". I would've conjured Shania Twain or something a little more savvy, but that might boost me up too much. What happens with sassy music is you get floated away from yourself, then snap back to reality too hard. I hate that. The only antidote is to just stay depressed.' It's there, too, in Anne Tyler's *Breathing Lessons*, an Everyman song sung by an Everyman as he brings in the laundry; and it crops up in the second series of *Ozark*.

Of course, one may have thought that a song so fetishised may have become meta over the years, either by a process of accretion or simply because of its popularity. Over time this has happened to 'My Way', has happened to 'Don't Stop Believin'', has happened to 'Mamma Mia', but there is nothing ironic or cute about 'Wichita Lineman', and in spite of its iconic status it has somehow remained pure.

The other obvious way in which songs have been given a new lease of life is through hip-hop sampling, and in this way various Guilty Pleasures have, over the years, developed a redemptive quality; this has happened to everyone from Spandau Ballet and Phil Collins to Hall & Oates and Steely Dan. 'Wichita' has largely escaped this. Ghostface Killah's 'Pokerface', produced by K. Flack a few years ago, used a sample of Sunday's Child's 1970 version, while more recently the young Wichita rapper XV and the producer Just Blaze – who is most famous for his work with Jay-Z – assembled the track using samples of the Dells' version.

'Wichita Lineman' is one of the very first examples of what would one day become known as Americana – which, as David Hepworth describes it, is anything written or sung by a white American that mentions a city or a highway, a term intended to reflect the fact that the people who like country music don't like the idea of country music. Country music can be sentimental and mawkish, but as soon as you step out of the genre, emotions become more abstract, more nuanced, more rounded. The difference between country and Americana is the difference between *Happy Days* and *American Graffiti*, between Radio 2 and Radio 6 Music, between a cowboy hat and a beard.

The song also became popular with what I rather facetiously referred to a few years ago as 'Woodsmen', those bearded and rather earnest musicians in lumberjack shirts and scowls who talked wistfully of remote cabins in north-western Wisconsin or renovated chicken shacks in the Californian woods, singers of indeterminate age who back in the noughties fronted bands of sullen subordinates who couldn't quite believe how successful they were. For a while Woodsmen were everywhere. The big one was Bon Iver's Justin Vernon, followed in no particular order by the Decemberists, Fleet Foxes, Arcade Fire, Great Lake Swimmers, Beirut, Band of Horses, Volcano Choir, Iron & Wine, My Morning Jacket, Calexico and all the rest. When the *New Yorker* published a piece about My Morning Jacket, they said, 'You know these guys are bearded without seeing a photograph of them.'

Johnny Cash covered 'Wichita', too, towards the end of his life. 'One person can't save another person, but almost,' Rosanne Cash once said about her father meeting the producer Rick Rubin. The union between the former hip-hop producer and the veteran country singer in the early nineties resulted in six *American Recordings* albums (plus a box set of outtakes) that completely revitalised Cash. The records re-established him both because of the material he covered and the way in which he was portrayed – warts and all. 'Wichita Lineman' appeared on the fourth album, *American IV: The Man Comes Around*, with Cash sounding for all the world like a man who had spent his life waiting to sing this song. At this stage in his career it was impossible to capture any hope in Cash's voice, only experience, but then that's why the records were so successful.

'When you listen to the material that he recorded with Rick Rubin, you can hear the life he's led, how his voice was affected by the drugs he took, especially on "Wichita Lineman",' said Peter Lewry, the editor of the Johnny Cash magazine *The Man in Black*. 'In the Fifties artists would take pills to stay awake and then go to sleep because of the hectic touring schedule. John turned to pills but unlike most artists, John became dependent on them. Not a day went by when he wasn't taking pills, and he was arrested for smuggling pills into the country and his life was on a downward spiral by the mid-Sixties to late Sixties. In fact, in a lot of programmes you see he looks so ill that a lot of people are amazed that he ever survived the Sixties. It was a struggle for him at the end. He worked hard on the songs, I mean he was even getting to the point where he couldn't record a whole song, they'd have to piece it together because he would struggle with breathing. He was in a wheelchair at the end, but he'd go into the studio every day. His voice in the last few years has a raw edge and especially with "Wichita Lineman", which in my opinion was much better than Glen Campbell's version, more feeling in it – I think he puts the story over better, and maybe that's down to John's life, the hard life that he lived. He just seemed to put an edge on it.'

The Johnny Cash version doesn't make for much of a karaoke song, although the original has proved to be more robust in this guise than you might imagine. Logically, it shouldn't be a karaoke song, and certainly not a successful one. As most karaoke interpretations are usually based on the best-known version of the song, and as Glen Campbell is such an accomplished singer, it's surprising that so many people think they can get away with singing it. 'My Way' doesn't bring the same problems, because all you really need to do is talk your way through it. Neither does 'Don't Stop Believin", which you can basically shout.* The same

---

* If you are ever asked about television's greatest moment, there obviously can be only one answer: the final two minutes of the final episode of *The Sopranos* (first shown on 10 June 2007). In this scene, when Tony Soprano glances upwards and the screen falters and turns to black many of us thought our Sky+ facility had decided to implode at the least opportune moment in TV history. Although as the credits began to roll we realised that this was perhaps the only way for David Chase's epic family saga to extinguish itself. Chase says that the show's audience was always bifurcated, and that on one sofa you had a small army who only wanted to see the Bada Bing mob whack people, while on the other you had another bunch who were far more interested in the family dynamic.

'I sort of knew that the people who wanted the big bloodbath at the end were not going to be thrilled with the ending, but what I did not realise was how angry those people would get,' said Chase. 'And it was amazing how long it went on. Especially when you figure that we had a rather significant war going on.'

Ultimately, the show's finale was all about the conflict. The theme of the final episode, no. 86, was 'Made in America', as much of a reference to Iraq as it was to the financial discomfort zone many US citizens found themselves in. Chase says he didn't want to be didactic about it, but all we needed to know about the subtext was there on Tony and Carmela's faces, when their son AJ tells them he wants to join up. And the final song in the final episode of the greatest television show ever made, the record that will forever be synonymous with closure? Journey's 'Don't Stop Believin", the hugely successful single from their 1981 album *Escape*. Which certainly confused the hell out of me.

'It didn't take much time at all to pick it, but there was a lot of conversation after the fact,' said Chase. 'I did something I'd never done before: in the location van, with the crew, I was saying, "What do you think?" When I said, "'Don't Stop Believin'"," people went, "What? Oh my god!" I said, "I know, I know, just give a listen," and little by little, people started coming around.' When the episode was aired, reactions to the denouement were mixed. 'I hear some people were very angry, and others were not,' said Chase. 'Which is what I expected.'

Since then, 'Don't Stop Believin" has become a karaoke classic, as popular

can be said of any ABBA song, as all you're really doing is repeating the words in a very loud voice, which isn't so different from singing a terrace chant at a football match. 'Wichita Lineman', though . . . well, that requires some pipes, requires a person to limber up before running up to it. Seriously, are you ready to attempt the plaintive denouement that is the song's final line? Yet still they come, these men and women whose need to be associated with the song, whose need to be seen choosing the song supersedes any ability they might have for actually completing the exercise successfully.

The first time I heard a semi-public rendition of the song was in the Groucho Club, in London's Dean Street, sometime in the early nineties. It was late at night, and a bunch of us had tumbled in there after an awards ceremony either to celebrate a much-deserved win or offset the injustice of losing. Having loitered at the bar, I had missed the rump of our party disappearing into another part of the club, the part where the piano player held court. It was his job to add some sweetness to the night by accessorising the evening with instrumental versions of whatever took his fancy, frankly. Essentially, he was a cocktail pianist, but

---

as any ABBA or Take That song. Journey's lead singer, Steve Perry, initially refused to let Chase use the song until he knew the fate of the leading characters, and didn't give final approval until three days before the episode aired. He feared that the song would be remembered as the soundtrack to Tony's demise, until Chase assured him that this would not be the case. Strangely, he was right. In 2009, it was performed in the pilot episode of the hit US TV series *Glee*, and for a while was the best-selling digital song not released in the twenty-first century.

when you consider the kind of cocktails that are popular in the Groucho – the espresso martini, the Negroni, anything containing at least two shots of absinthe – you understand how inadequate that description might be. Pianists in the Groucho could play you Sinatra's hits, if they so desired, or a little light Bacharach, although they were happiest when exploring the rather more esoteric tributaries of popular song.

So I was surprised when I heard the rest of my gang suddenly burst into song, hurtling through Jimmy Webb's convoluted lyrics, as the pianist, who was predictably far less emboldened by strong drink than they were, vamped behind them – half a bar behind them, to be exact.

'How could this be?' I thought to myself. Surely I was the only person who knew this song? Surely I was the only one melancholic enough to have memorised the words? Well, apparently not. I repeated this exercise dozens of times – maybe even hundreds of times – over the next few years, often with one of the original culprits (Robin, Simon, Alex, Tris, Oliver, Robert, etc.), and frequently bolstered by a random newspaper editor, politician or bold-face name who had made the mistake of turning up that evening. ('Glen Campbell is an honorary Irishman,' said my friend Oliver. 'When I grew up, every show band played it, every pub played it . . . We all thought it was an Irish song.') Giving an impassioned, drunken, melodramatic version of Jimmy Webb's most famous song at an hour when most right-thinking members had already slipped into the night, homeward bound, became something of a rite of passage. Simon, who was always one of the most enthusiastic participants – if not always one of the most accomplished – used to say that one of the rules he lived by was knowing that it was time to go home whenever anyone started singing 'American Pie'. It didn't take long to realise that Don McLean's iconic shopping list of a song had been replaced. If only Simon had listened to his own advice.

After a while, having spontaneously performed it in hotel bars and restaurants all over the world, it became easy to sing, the only line that might cause me to falter being the one about that stretch down south. What I soon learned was that you have to attack that stanza as though it might never end, singing it out in the same way you breathe into one of those machines at the doctor's that are designed to judge your lung capacity, because to try and add nuance when you don't know the song very well is only going to cause you heartache, perhaps more than even Jimmy Webb imagined.

According to Alex James, Blur's redoubtable bass player, the Groucho was 'a proudly exclusive, sugary cocktail of celebrity, money, frocks and genius'. In the nineties, it was run largely by women, the fiercest of whom was Gordana, who was not only the most feared manageress, but also the staff member who would berate James most often. 'You can't keep riding that bicycle down the stairs,' she would shout. 'Someone is going to get hurt. What? Well, I'm not surprised you've got a sore leg. You're a bloody idiot! And if you want to pay the pianist five hundred pounds to play "Wichita Lineman" for an hour, get him to come round to your house to do it.'

Somewhat by default, it became my own karaoke song of choice, beating off competition from 'On Days Like This' by Matt Monro or Bobby Darin's 'Beyond the Sea'. I'd sung 'True' by Spandau Ballet, attempted 'I'm Your Puppet' by James and Bobby Purify, 'Hold On, I'm Coming' by Sam & Dave and 'Angels' by Robbie Williams, as well as 'Same Old Saturday Night' and 'Learnin' the Blues' (both made famous by Sinatra), but it was always 'Wichita' I came back to, like a haunting refrain.

Someone who loves the song even more than Alex James is the club's resident pianist, Rod Melvin. Rod has been playing the piano at the Groucho since 1995, having previously worked at the Zanzibar, Le Pont de la Tour, L'Escargot, the Lexington and various other clubs and restaurants in London. Along with Ian Dury he is a former member of Kilburn and the High Roads, and in his time has played with Brian Eno, Tony Visconti and the Moodies. Hired by the general manager Mary-Lou Sturridge, and encouraged by her then partner, Hamish Stuart from the Average White Band, Melvin started doing the late shift, mixing classics with personal favourites, 'Didn't We' and 'Wichita Lineman' included. 'Mary-Lou started allowing people to sing around the piano, so people would come in, late at night, and join in,' said Rod. 'Then one night [the journalist] Simon Kelner came in, started singing "Wichita

Lineman", and a tradition started. Suddenly I was playing it three times a week.'

For Melvin, it is a joy to play. 'Some tunes you don't tire of playing over and over again, and in this case it's the combination of the chords and the melody. Even if I'm not singing, it's a very visual song. When you start playing those opening chords, and you get that first melody, there's something about the space. I always get pictures. You know in movies when you get those scenes of roads going through fields for miles? It's like that, with these telegraph poles, something about that spaciousness, of someone alone in this vast space. It goes into another key, in the middle, which is significant, I think. Because different keys have different feels. So the first half is quite sad, but has beautiful chords. Then it shifts. The song doesn't start or finish on the root key, which is very unusual. For a simple song it's incredibly complex, a little like Randy Newman. You can tell that once it starts to become predictable, Jimmy Webb veers off in another direction. "Up, Up and Away" is another complex song. As for "MacArthur Park", how would you come up with that? It's crazy. And that line, "I need you more than want you . . .", it's very economical in its use of words to convey what it does. Jimmy Webb said the Beatles influenced him when they did "Penny Lane", by using place names, and having a cinematic sweep. It's incredibly sad. God, it just gets you from the first line. And then it keeps getting better.'

He often segues into David Bowie's 'Starman', making a virtue of the Morse code coda, 'which works brilliantly if you do it properly. Get it wrong and you've ruined two songs.'

In 2010, I went to see Glen Campbell perform at London's Festival Hall. He looked trim, appeared to have all his own hair (he was seventy-four at the time) and could still execute the difficult parts of his songs. His band was more than adequate, and the arrangements of his hits were in accordance with the records. Of course, he left 'Wichita Lineman' till last, and what a thing of great beauty it was. The arrangement was identical to the one he had used on Jools Holland's *Later . . .* a few years previously, which made the song sound modern, while being respectful to the original. I was moved, nearly teary, and afterwards decided to go to the Groucho Club for a nightcap. Bizarrely, it was the first night in living memory that Roddy wasn't playing it on the piano.

'I met a well-known photographer one night in the Groucho who lives in LA and who knows Jimmy Webb really well,' said Melvin. 'He loves his music so much he used to go round to his house and lie under the piano when he played. I don't know anyone who loves the song more than Alex James, though. Along with "Up, Up and Away" and "California Girls" and "God Only Knows" by the Beach Boys, he'd be very happy for me never to play anything else.'

Like Burt Bacharach, Brian Wilson had the ability to mix euphoria and melancholia in the space of a single song, often in the same melody, and occasionally in the same note.

165

Given his history of personal problems (an aggressive and belligerent father, a dysfunctional family, a fragile mental state, addictions, weight problems and a long-standing overbearing therapist), it's hardly surprising that Wilson's best music always had an innate sadness, a tender quality, which can be found in such diverse Beach Boys songs as 'Our Prayer', 'Wind Chimes', 'The Lonely Sea', 'Melt Away', 'Guess I'm Dumb' (the song he recorded with Glen Campbell), 'Surf's Up', 'The Warmth of the Sun' (written in response to the JFK assassination) and his greatest triumph, 'Till I Die' (a version of which appears on their 1971 LP *Surf's Up*, though a vastly superior extended instrumental version was released on *Endless Harmony* in 1998). As legendary rock journalist Nick Kent has so eloquently written, Wilson wrote 'harmonies so complex, so graceful they seemed to have more in common with a Catholic Mass than any cocktail acapella doo-wop'. Wilson called his work 'rock church music', while every one of his classic songs contains a 'money chord'. Mark Rothko, eat your heart out.

The remarkable thing that Wilson achieved was to create a world that wasn't there before, a world that not only celebrated a Californian dream world, but also invented an inner world where Wilson – and anyone who ever listened to a Wilson record – could go and be comforted. In this case his music acted as medication, therapy or, in Wilson's case, a piano standing in a box full of sand. The other remarkable thing is the way in which Wilson's world connected with so many millions of people. The awful irony of his fabulous invention was his complete inability to enjoy it himself, even though it gave so much enjoyment to so many others. In Barney Hoskyns's gripping book *Waiting for the Sun: Strange Days, Weird Scenes and the Sound of Los Angeles*, Jimmy Webb said, 'I don't think that the Californian myth, the dream that a few of us touched, would have happened without Brian, but I don't think Brian would have happened without the dream.' Wilson fuelled a fantasy, and surf pop was born.

The Californian coast is a celebration of fantasy, a Pacific kingdom of sunshine, sand and surf, a reconstructed world of wonder where plastic palm trees sway beneath artificial moons, and where David Hockney paintings come to life. This post-industrial landscape aspires to be a terrestrial paradise, a near-tropical dreamland where vistas of magnificent natural beauty vie with car parks littered with neo-Mexican shopping malls, where giant redwoods and valleys of golden poppies surround the state's popular cathedrals of kitsch. This is a life of abundance, where anything is possible and little is real. A lot of California looks like a grandiose campsite, a frontier state where much looks as though it were thrown up overnight. Here, little looks permanent, making the landscape look as untamed as it looks manicured. But there are few things more enjoyable than hurtling down the Pacific Coast Highway in a rented convertible, few things better than the Californian sun hitting your Ermanno Scervino sunglasses, the spray from the surf hitting your windscreen, the wind rushing across your face and the sound of the Beach Boys blasting through the in-car stereo. For California, Brian Wilson always had unlimited praise.

As did Jimmy Webb.

When we describe the way music makes us feel, it's often got something to do with abandon – feeling completely separate, cut off, falling through the air, walking through the woods, flying way above everyone, standing on the cliffs looking at the midnight ocean, crouching in a cornfield and peering into the valley . . . Levitating.

One of my least successful book ideas – when I told my agent about it, he told me to go and have a long lie-down – was a music and travel book identifying the best soundtracks to listen to in various places around the world. I thought this was a brilliant wheeze, an encyclopaedia of great road songs, awesome beach ballads, soaring urban anthems (lots of Clash, U2 and, yes, even Billy Idol) and the exact Kraftwerk tunes you'd need for a ten-day skiing holiday in the Alps. Yet there is no record that evokes a landscape more powerfully than 'Wichita Lineman'. It is not just that the guitar line sounds so nomadic, it is the imagery the song conjures up: the imagery of Ed Ruscha, of electricity cables black against silkscreen cornflower, the imagery of small towns, big towns in the fifties and sixties – a cluttered horizon full of billboards, traffic signs, fast-food neons, gas stations and, yes, telegraph poles.

It's perhaps not wise to contradict someone like Pablo Picasso, but on this occasion I have no choice. 'Painting

is not done to decorate apartments,' he said in 1945. 'It is
an instrument of war.' He was referring, obliquely, to his
enormous canvas capturing the agony when the Luftwaffe
and the Italian Aviazione Legionaria, at General Franco's
behest, carpet-bombed the Basque town of Guernica. Yet
on the subject of painting, Picasso was just about as wrong
as a genius can be. Social commentary is a spectrum, and
not every work of art has the ambition of *Guernica*, just as
not every song wants to kick-start a revolution. Painting, in
common with all of the arts, invariably acts as a second- or
third-hand accompaniment or counterpoint to its locale, a
way of lifting the spirits in a darkened room or giving a
Caribbean sunset extra gravitas. In some cases it's designed
to fit into the service lifts of Upper East Side apartment
blocks, and in others it's designed to sit in the lobbies of
large Swiss banks. It's why we buy prints of famous paintings, why wallpaper was developed and why furniture
designers now have egos the size of George Sherlock sofas.

This is particularly true of music. While pop records
that aspire to great art could conceivably be listened to
anywhere, a lot of very good pop music has the effect of
making a landscape look even grander than it does already,
making a blue sky appear even richer, painting a suburban
landscape in the correct hues of fifties Americana or under-
scoring the intensity of a Chicago backstreet. Great pop
music, whether it was designed to or not, expresses an abne-
gation of responsibility. And this is especially true if you
are on holiday or at leisure – that moment when a searing

power-chord shooting across a cloudless sky fills your heart with whatever you want it to or encourages you to lean your foot a little more heavily on the accelerator pedal. If you've ever chosen the scenic drive home, then you'll know the feeling.

Which means, I suppose, that music can also be a decorative art. While many of us buy records because we have a fundamental attachment to the preoccupations of the people who make them – when we're young, at least, or pretending we still are – at other times we buy them simply because we happen to like the way they sound: they encourage us to engage with our surroundings, but also allow us to distance ourselves from them.

If you're driving just north of Los Angeles, say, climbing up the Pacific Coast Highway on your way to Santa Barbara, hearing 'Sleepwalk' by Santo & Johnny will not only transport you out of California, it might just lift you right into outer space. Music and landscape make perfect bedfellows. John Peel's perfect dovetail of sound and vision appears on page 153 of his part-autobiography, *Margrave of the Marshes*. It is 1961, and Peel is driving from New Orleans back to Dallas. 'The drive gave me one of the greatest musical moments of my life. I had been driving for some time and it must have been two or three in the morning as I started through the richly forested area of East Texas known as Piney Woods.' There was hardly any traffic on the road, and as the highway rose and fell through the trees, past tiny little towns that were barely shacks and shop fronts, 'the moon, which shone brilliantly directly in front of me, turned the concrete to silver'. Peel recalls that he was listening, as everyone did in that area at that time, to Wolfman Jack, the maverick DJ who broadcasted from a station called XERB, over the border in Mexico. The Wolfman was just about the most exotic man in pop back then (he is immortalised, for those that care, in George Lucas's love letter to the period, *American Graffiti*), and as Peel came over the top of yet another hill 'to see another tiny town below me, he played Elmore James's "Stranger Blues" and I knew that I would never forget the perfect conjunction of place, mood and music. Nor have I.'

For music and landscape to co-exist in a perfect state, everything needs to work in 5.1 surround sound, the sort that makes you jump when the drums come in, the sort that sends you careering down a ravine after a particularly notable key change. For me, that notion of perfection is usually embodied by John Barry, Burt Bacharach or the Beach Boys – especially their more maudlin music – and the golden dunes of California. I close my eyes and I could be kicking sand on Malibu beach; clench them a little tighter and I'm transported right into a Rousseau painting, walking between 2D tigers and childlike palm trees.

Like Burt Bacharach's lyricist Hal David, Jimmy Webb relished images of mobility and movement – cars, highways, trains, even balloons – as well as all the telegraph poles from here to the horizon. Cars would become an obsession for Webb, and central to his songwriting. When

171

he became rich – and he became rich almost as soon as he became famous – one of the first things he did was buy himself some automobiles.

In 2017, as he was being chauffeured by *GQ*'s motoring editor Jason Barlow in a McLaren 570S Spider to a gig he was about to play at St James's Church in London's Piccadilly, Webb waxed lyrical about his vintage AC Cobra – bought directly from legendary racing driver Carroll Shelby, the man who created the Cobra, one of the most genuinely iconic cars ever made.

'You could actually drive in those days,' he said. 'Once you hit the Nevada state line, there was no speed limit, it was like being on the autobahn. I'd run that thing up to 120, 130 mph. It was terrifyingly easy. But then it would start doing a little dance, so I was never that keen to see how fast it would *really* go. All it would take would be to drop a tyre on that soft shoulder on the freeway and I'd be a firework. It would have ensured my everlasting fame, I guess.'

He was talking about 1968, the year he made it, the year he came into some serious money. He had another Cobra, and he had it on very good authority that it was originally built for Steve McQueen, but he turned it down. He thought it was too dangerous. Shelby sold it to Bill Cosby, who went out for a ride in it with his little daughter one day and said, 'Take it back.' It was too fast. Then it was sold to an Englishman who lived in California part of the time. One night, presumably after a few drinks, he drove it off the Pacific Coast Highway.

'In fact, I watched mine burn one day,' said Webb. 'It was a primeval device. The battery sat between the seats, but I was taking nice women out at the time, so I asked the guys in the shop to move it into the boot, in a bracket with safety cables to keep the bracket vertical. Made it into a Californian dragster, basically. I said to my brother, "You ought to feel the acceleration in second gear, man." So I did that one day to show him, and the car blew up. The battery had detached, and whatever fuel vapour was in there ignited, and it went up. Took out my left eyebrow in the process. We grabbed garden hoses out of the neighbours' yards. I don't know what the hell we thought we were doing, it was already an inferno. But I rebuilt it. I put sixty grand into it.'

As a road song, 'By the Time I Get to Phoenix' doesn't bear much scrutiny where the timings are concerned, and there are some people who have even produced maps to show how improbable they are, but as Webb said himself, 'Sometimes as a writer you come to a decision like that and you just flip a coin. You could try "By the Time I Get to Flagstaff", but does it work as well?' One such person approached him one night after a concert, 'And he showed me how it was impossible for me to drive from LA to Phoenix, and then how far it was to Albuquerque. In short, he told me, "This song is impossible." And so it is. It's a kind of fantasy about something I wish I would have done, and it sort of takes place in a twilight zone of reality.'

The car would be emblematic of America's aspirations in the fifties and sixties. Every new Cadillac had to outdo and outgrow the previous model. Each car had acres of chrome and dozens of winking lights, like a mobile juke-box. The 1959 Caddy had lethally sharp-looking tail fins, which had sprouted rocket-shaped tail lights that seemed to be clinging precariously to their sides. The Cadillac, like much music of the time, was a prime example of what the American design critic Thomas Hine defined as 'populuxe', a fifties aesthetic that fused populism with luxury. 'The decade was one of America's great shopping sprees,' he said. 'Never before were so many people able to acquire so many things, and never before was there such a choice.' It was the era of the newly created world of mass suburbia, where everything family-owned – the house, the car, the furniture, the hi-fi (on which to play your Dean Martin and Frank Sinatra records) – was provisional; even if it didn't wear out, one always had the hope of being able to move up the ladder to something better. 'There were so many new things to buy – a power mower, a more modern dinette set, a washing machine with a window through which you could see the wash water turn a disgusting grey, a family room, a two-toned refrigerator, a charcoal grill, and, of course, televisions.' Or a Jet Age Cadillac, each year, every year.

In America in the fifties, suburbia determined popular culture, and in some part of their being every suburbanite wanted a new car. This was the decade of the automobile, when America took to the roads with a vengeance, exploiting the highways and driving anywhere just for the hell of it. Which is why it's not at all surprising that the fifties and sixties produced so many songs about cars. Jimmy Webb certainly wrote his fair share: 'By the Time I Get to Phoenix' is just one long, convoluted road trip, while 'Wichita Lineman' is written completely from the perspective of someone in a car moving slowly along a country backroad.

As David Hepworth once pointed out, many of us have internalised the names of places referenced in the Great American Songbook, at least those concerned with moving from country to city, from city to city, 'and from the city back to the theoretical peace of rural life'. These migrations, both large and small, are what we expect to hear about in a lot of American music, whether it charts the movement along Route 66, Chuck Berry's 'Promised Land' or even the geographical impossibilities of 'By the Time I Get to Phoenix'. We can remember them all: Memphis, Tulsa, Pasadena, Chattanooga, Birmingham, Georgia, San Francisco, San Jose, Muscle Shoals, Asbury Park, Rockaway Beach, Highway 61, 53rd and 3rd, (coast to coast) LA to Chicago, Tucson to Tucumcari, and even the New Jersey Turnpike, which is obviously one of the first places one should go to look for America.

'To any foreigner who grew up hearing "Chattanooga Choo-Choo" and "I've Got a Gal in Kalamazoo", American towns are the most musical on the planet,' wrote Mark Steyn.

The Mason–Dixon Line has been responsible for many songs which deal with its figurative significance, not least Lynyrd Skynyrd's 'Sweet Home Alabama'. Written in

1973 as a response to two songs by Neil Young, 'Southern Man' and 'Alabama', which dealt with racism and slavery in the South, Skynyrd's almost reactionary retort was both a putdown of Young and a celebration of the band's heritage. Acknowledged as a *chanson de revanche*, in a wider and more contemporary context it can be seen as analogous to the espousal of Trumpian politics, or at least the insidious nature of Trumpian beliefs. When Ronnie Van Zant, the band's lead singer, defiantly says that Watergate doesn't bother him, he was not only bemoaning the liberal obsession with Nixon, but also speaking for the entire South, asking that they should not to be judged as individuals for the racial problems of southern society in the same way they wouldn't judge ordinary northerners for the failures of their leaders in Washington.

In some respects, 'Sweet Home Alabama' is a populist anthem, the kind of broadly drawn broadside that should appeal to those who like their ideologies reduced to slogans. But then by definition any successful protest song condenses an argument into a chorus. It is perhaps surprising that there have been so few contemporary populist anthems – are there any? – as well as so few anti-populist songs; after all, a world in which Donald Trump, Brexit and Matteo Salvini have thrived ought to have emboldened those on both sides of the divide. Of course, it is untrue to say that the protest song is no longer a cultural force, as hip hop has been criticising government, shouting (literally) about social injustice and addressing the ubiquity of police brutality in black communities since the late seventies (which is why Public Enemy's Chuck D famously dubbed hip hop 'the black CNN' all those years ago), but hip hop has almost become a protest genre in its own right, and so in many people's eyes is less influential.

The writers of 'Sweet Home Alabama' long denied that it was a white supremacist anthem, insisting that the lyrics were more ambivalent; and while this might be true, it remains an unusually powerful invocation.

'Wichita Lineman' is anything but.

Los Angeles has always had an abundance of cultural entry points, but for me it's forever associated with one image: the photograph – taken by Terry O'Neill – of Elton John on the blue-carpeted stage at Dodger Stadium in 1975. Elton, wearing a sequined Dodgers baseball kit, is sitting at his piano, which is also covered in blue carpet, and is about to launch into 'Benny and the Jets' in front of the 80,000-strong crowd. The picture is so vivid you almost expect it to start playing the song, like a musical birthday card.

At the time, Elton was the biggest star in the world, and his two shows at the home of the LA Dodgers that year were the pinnacle of his early success. As the DJ Paul Gambaccini once said, no single photograph better demonstrates the hold a rock star can have over the public.

'Benny and the Jets' is also the quintessential LA record, and you can guarantee you'll hear it on the radio whenever you visit the city. You'll also hear every other great seventies song. Most of the great 'landscape' driving music was made in the seventies, so it feels completely natural when the likes of America's 'Ventura Highway', the Doobie Brothers' 'Long Train Runnin'' or Lynyrd Skynyrd's 'Free Bird' come hurtling out of the rental car's speakers – accompanied, of course, by a flash of neon light, a plume of purple smoke and a wash of dry ice.

Some say that Los Angeles is just New York lying down, although it's a hell of a lot younger; in fact, in LA, by the time you're thirty-five you're older than most of the buildings. You'll certainly be older than the cars, because LA is the most car-obsessed city in the world. (It was once said that the cars are so cool in Hollywood that children there don't wear masks on Halloween; instead, they usually dress up as valet parkers.) And if you haven't got a white Range Rover or a Mercedes S65, then frankly you're nobody.

There are more cars in California than people in any of the other states of the US, while LA's freeway system handles over twelve million cars on a daily basis. The lucky residents of LA County spend an estimated four days of each year stuck in traffic. Everything revolves around the car here (why else would someone open an all-night drive-in taxidermist?), and whereas most European films usually involve a small boy and a bicycle, all decent American films involve a car chase.

There are now so many purpose-built digital radio stations that it's possible to choose what you want to listen to for any journey, whether it's exclusively music made in the nineties or the thirties. On a recent trip to LA, as I drove through Bel Air, past the mansions and the gate lodges of Beverly Hills, the exotic Chandleresque haciendas, rustling palms, lawn sprinklers and chirruping crickets, and up into the Hollywood Hills (where it's still possible, if you're wearing a patchwork denim waistcoat and a pair of purple velvet loon pants, to catch a whiff of 1972 patchouli oil, joss stick and body odour), I found a station pumping out an assortment of Elton John songs, including a few from one of his semi-great forgotten albums of the seventies, *Rock of the Westies*. This is the great lost Elton record, an alternative *Goodbye Yellow Brick Road*, an uneven but fascinating album containing half a dozen classic songs: 'I Feel Like a Bullet (In the Gun of Robert Ford)', 'Dan Dare (Pilot of the Future)', 'Feed Me', 'Street Kids', 'Grow Some Funk of Your Own', etc.

As I listened to the songs in my car, gunning it down Sunset Boulevard with the midday sun and the palms above me, I felt myself being transported back to the LA of the mid-seventies. Suddenly I was driving through a bright blue Hockney dreamscape, surrounded by CinemaScope billboards for *Shampoo*, *Tommy* and *One Flew Over the Cuckoo's Nest*. All of a sudden my trouser bottoms got a little wider, my lapels turned into aircraft carriers, my cologne became a little more pronounced, my shoes sprouted three-inch stack heels and my denim waistcoat was suddenly made of silver lamé. Oh, and guess what? I was now sporting a pair of tinted spectacles the size of Texas. There was a copy of *Rolling Stone* on the passenger seat, along with a packet of More cigarettes, a paperback of Robert Pirsig's *Zen and the Art of Motorcycle Maintenance* and an eight-track cartridge of Supertramp's *Crisis? What Crisis?*

The one California song I've never particularly cared for is its most famous. In fact, I've always found the idea for the song more interesting than the record itself. Written by Don Felder, Glenn Frey and Don Henley, 'Hotel California' is ostensibly a song about materialism and excess, written during a decade when California was no longer simply being portrayed as a daydream pleasuredome and was starting to be used as a metaphor for indulgence and ennui. Henley has excused the song hundreds of times, principally describing it as a snapshot of the excesses of American culture and the uneasy balance between art and commerce. 'Everyone wants to know what this song means,' he said. 'I know, it's so boring. It's a song about the dark underbelly of the American Dream.' Like so many songs written about California in the seventies, it was a song about an outsider's journey from innocence to experience.

Bernie Leadon was the only band member at the time who was from the state (Timothy B. Schmit, who joined in 1977, was also from California). Don Henley was from Texas, Joe Walsh from New Jersey, Randy Meisner from Nebraska, Glenn Frey from Detroit and Don Felder from Florida. Felder said this about the song: 'As you're driving in Los Angeles at night, you can see the glow of the energy and the lights of Hollywood and Los Angeles for 100 miles out in the desert. And on the horizon, as you're driving in, all of these images start coming into your mind of the propaganda and advertisement you've experienced about California. In other words, the movie stars, the stars on Hollywood Boulevard, the beaches, bikinis, palm trees, all those images that you see and that people think of when they think of California start running through your mind. You're anticipating that. That's all you know of California.'

Don Henley put it another way: 'We were all middle-class kids from the Midwest. "Hotel California" was our interpretation of the high life in Los Angeles.'

The temporality of places such as New York or Miami is what makes them so exciting, so operative, so full of movement. Wichita, in our imagination at least, is always there. When Jimmy Webb writes, 'And if it snows that stretch down south / won't ever stand the strain,' he knows it, and because of that we know it too. This is always going to be the case: that stretch down south is always going to be there. The song immerses itself in the wilderness of the Midwestern imagination, a liberation from all that is not wild.

One wonders how big a city has to be, or how small a town, to have a song written about it. By now, most state capitals must have had a song written about them (with the exception of Juneau and Annapolis, obviously), and even the most inconsequential conurbations have popped up in songs by the kings and queens of Americana and been celebrated by the finest minds in alt.country.

Randy Newman's 'Baltimore' first appeared on his 1977 album *Little Criminals*, with the narrator being a disaffected citizen of the city bemoaning the hard times that had resulted in a sharp decline in the quality of life there. It's vague social commentary, a hastily written post-mortem, but it's beautiful. No, not everyone in Baltimore liked it – online message boards are still full of withering insults, my favourite being, 'Go sodomise yourself with a chainsaw, Randy Newman' – yet it very quickly began to be regarded as one of Newman's very best songs. Melancholy lyrics, a hypnotic piano riff and a plaintive vocal make for one extraordinarily maudlin travelogue, one that could easily be called 'Chicago', 'New Orleans' or 'The Bronx'. Or indeed, these days, even neighbourhoods in San Francisco or Santa Barbara. *Time* magazine got it right when it said that Newman the lyricist is a refreshing irritant. 'And Newman the composer is a sweet seducer. His music is a lush amalgam of Americana.' Or chalk and cheese in the same bun.

Just a few years after I eventually learned to drive, I organised a road trip across the US with one of my very best friends, Robin, a journey that would take us all the way from New York, Philadelphia and Washington down through the Blue Ridge Mountains, Nashville and Memphis, before joining Route 66 and continuing on to LA, via Texas, Arizona, New Mexico and Nevada. And of course, I made an individual mix tape for every state, starting off on the Eastern Seaboard with lots of Bruce Springsteen, Bob Seger, Southside Johnny and Tom Petty, before moving into the southern states with plenty of Neville Brothers, Dr John and Allen Toussaint, and then joining the dustbowl motorway accompanied by fairly generic seventies FM rock – the Steve Miller Band, the Eagles, Foghat, Boston and some more Tom Petty. Like feathers on a freeway, Petty's songs are meant to bounce around your car as you cruise down the highway on a journey to the past. Built on a sound based on the Big Jangle, they actively encourage nostalgia, songs you're meant to play as you're driving home from work, or out into the desert, or back to the sixties. Some would say he was celebrated for using nostalgia as a survival tool, but I had to have his songs on my tapes.

It seemed imperative to have the Eagles, too. For many of my generation, at a certain point in our development they were the band that we loved to hate more than anyone else. When I was at art school in the late seventies, admitting you liked the Eagles was tantamount to admitting that you not only knew nothing about music, but also that you probably harboured a secret desire to light joss sticks and cover yourself in patchouli oil. Worse, it hinted that you may have been slightly more interested in cruising down Ventura Highway in an open-top Mustang rather than slumming it at the back of some dirty nightclub above a pub on the outskirts of Basildon.

Even so, in preparing for our road trip I had failed to understand that the radio stations in the States are built for long journeys, and that the soundtrack to my journey would be supplied whether I liked it or not. There was no need for me to make a cassette compilation of Steely Dan's 'King of the World', Robert Plant's 'Big Log' or Neil

Young's 'Powderfinger', as they – and everything else I'd recorded for the journey – were being played on the radio every half an hour anyway.

'Good job you recorded this,' deadpanned Robin as we trundled through New Mexico, after we'd listened to 'Take It Easy' by the Eagles, 'because they've only played it six times on the radio today.'

'Take It Easy' mentions Winslow, Arizona, and it was just outside Winslow that we found the journey's own Holy Grail. The sun was falling in the sky, promising a rich, dark sunset as we sped along the highway towards Two Guns. In the distance the Juniper Mountains cut across the horizon like tears of pale-blue tissue paper. As we gunned towards them we looked to our left and saw a deserted drive-in, standing forlorn in the dirt, casting shadows that stretched all the way back to town. Suddenly I felt like an extra in *American Graffiti*, sitting in the custom-built bench seat of a hot rod, my cap-sleeved right arm around my girl, my ducktail brushing the rear-view mirror and Del Shannon's 'Runaway' pouring through the dashboard speaker.

Here was the true spirit of Route 66 in all its faded glory. Like the highway itself, the Tonto Drive-In was a totem of America's glorious past, a testament to the new frontier, the freedom to travel and the democratised automotive dream of the fifties, when a car was still every American's birth-right. This deserted cathedral, standing stoic and proud in the burnt sienna sunset, was, quite literally, the end of the road. Suddenly California – with all its promises of eternal youth and 'two girls for every boy' – seemed a long, long way away.

Of course, my epiphany was ably abetted by the tapes I'd made. We weren't hearing 'Wichita Lineman' every half an hour on the radio, nor were we blessed with 'Are You There (With Another Girl)?', 'On Days Like This', 'The Ipcress File' and all the other loungecore songs I'd recorded just for moments like this. So all my work had not actually been in vain.

A few years later, I was driving down the Californian coast from San Francisco to LA, and I listened to digital radio all the way, moving the dial through 'stations' that played music from every decade of the last eighty years. If I'd have driven long enough, I probably would have heard everything that's ever been recorded, from Louis Armstrong to CeeLo Green, from the Andrews Sisters to Tyler the Creator, from Big Bill Broonzy to Death Cab for Cutie. It was a joyous experience, but it could have been anyone's.

So the next time I did a Californian road trip, from LA to San Diego via Santa Monica and Palm Springs, the soundtrack was worked out in some detail: I started off with some Erin Bode and Nightmares on Wax, followed swiftly by Example, Midlake and Ed Sheeran, before moving on to Bon Iver, Here We Go Magic and Ducktails. Sure, I could simply have listened to the radio and probably enjoyed myself just as much. That wasn't the point. This was my journey and I was the one who was going to decide what it sounded like.

It's hardly surprising that journeys are often best accessorised by film soundtracks. By its very nature, the soundtrack is a supplementary medium. It's intrusive and indistinct by turns, following its film like a shadow. But if, as Steely Dan's Donald Fagen says, good music should sabotage expectations, then it would be easy to say that there is very little good music in the movies. Aural clichés are as widespread as visual ones: jazz for the city, narcissistic flutes in the suburbs; Aaron Copland-style orchestration for small-town Americana; scratchy guitars and piping horns for urban thrillers. For pastoral, copy Debussy; for devastation, rework Barber or Albinoni; for a western, hire Morricone (the man who put the opera into horse opera).

Once I even made my own. In the summer of 1990, I was in Carmel, in California, about to have dinner at Clint Eastwood's restaurant, the Hog's Head Inn (at the time he was the town's mayor). As I walked down through the centre of town, I passed one of those generic new-age shops, the ones that sell everything from joss sticks and expensively framed Grateful Dead posters to designer lava lamps and spa creams. It also sold various CDs of ocean sounds – Californian ocean sounds to boot. And as I had been in love with the idea of the Californian ocean from the age of about ten, I had to buy one.

And I bought it with one thing in mind. Almost as soon as I got home to London I put it into the CD player and then played one of my bespoke Beach Boys cassettes over the top, so I could listen to 'Surf's Up', 'Till I Die' and

'California Saga' with the sound of the Big Sur waves crashing against the rocks in the background. I had replicated almost completely my Californian experience – which was designed primarily so I could listen to a surf soundtrack ad nauseam as I drove along the Pacific Coast Highway in a rented Mustang – which meant that whenever I wanted to, I could take myself back to Route 101 and 'Cabinessence' without leaving the confines of west London. The Durutti Column's 'Sketch for Summer' has birdsong on it, as does Virginia Astley's 1983 mini-masterpiece *From Gardens Where We Feel Secure*, which comes complete with its own natural soundtrack, in the shape of field recordings of birdsong and sheep. There is a little light piano, some woodwind and some ambient vocals, but mainly this is the sound of the countryside, an instrumental accompaniment to a typical British summer's day. Some songs are even transfigurative, and whenever I hear 'Who Knows Where the Time Goes?' by Fairport Convention, I immediately sense I'm walking along a deserted British beach in the middle of winter, surrounded by little but cloud.

With 'Wichita Lineman' I'm still in that rented Mustang, bombing for the border.

6: THE BEAUTIFUL MUNDANE

> Reporter: Glen, have you played
> music all your life?
> Glen Campbell: Not yet.

Glen Campbell finished 1968 as the US's top-selling artist, outdistancing the Beatles by a considerable margin. That year, four of his albums sold over a million copies. In December alone, he accounted for over $4.5 million in LP sales. He picked up four Grammy awards, was named the Entertainer of the Year by Nashville's Country Music Association and somehow ended up as the honorary chairman of the National Arthritis Foundation. He was a genuine phenomenon. The Academy of Country and Western Music also named him the Best Male Vocalist of the Year and Top Television Personality, and presented him with an award for Best Album. He started 1969 with more of the same: television, movies, awards, state fairs, guest appearances, records, concerts.

It was Campbell's relationship with Jimmy Webb that made his career, and it was Webb's relationship with Campbell that made his. 'You need a good piece of poetry up front and then a great melody to go with it,' was Campbell's summation of Webb's genius. After 'Wichita Lineman', the pair would continue to work together, off and on, for years, with Campbell performing Webb's songs and both of them appearing together in concert; they even worked on an album together, *Reunion*, in 1974. In 1969, there had been that third town song, 'Galveston', written by Webb and performed by Campbell. The first two collaborations spun tales of journeys, love and longing, personalising the universal by juxtaposing the prosaic with the extraordinary. 'Galveston' was originally an anti-war song, until it was tweaked by Campbell to make it more ambiguous. He even appeared in a promotional video wearing a uniform, even though the line that resonates so much is the one in which he says he's afraid of dying.

As someone who understood the power of dissonance, it's ironic that Webb will probably be remembered most for his ability to add a little sweetness to the day, something he does so expertly in 'Galveston'. Here he persuades Campbell to elongate the name of the city, to give it some gravitas, to make it appear more romantic as well as more iconic. Even so, Webb was expecting to hear some Samuel Barber-type strings on the record, only to be disappointed by Campbell's rat-a-tat-tat let's-go-kick-their-ass arrangement. Still, it's hardly surprising that Webb often wants to sweeten his songs as well as novelise them; after all, for a man who is so sentimental and nostalgic about the expiration of grace from our way of life, home is of paramount importance to him, even more than it was when he was a lanky farmboy. In 'Galveston' he adopts the POV of a soldier who flashes back to romantic encounters by the Gulf to help get over his dread of dying in combat.

Not long after the song was a hit, Webb appeared in a street parade in the city, part of its shrimp festival (it is next door to Louisiana), and was pelted as he walked through the streets with his long hair, wearing a Pierre Cardin suit and an extravagant scarf. 'I was in the middle of a politically polarised situation,' he said. 'People didn't know how they felt about the song – is this guy a peacenik or what?' They would give him the keys to the city, so the act of acknowledgement was obviously more important than any ideological nuance.

Webb's original lyrics in the second verse were obviously anti-war, although in Campbell's version they were altered to become rather more patriotic. 'I'm not a writer, I'm really a "song doctor",' Campbell once said. 'If I hear a good song that I like, I'll change lines and chord progressions, and make it my own.'

Unsurprisingly, 'Galveston' became especially beloved by members of the armed services. According to Webb, the sailors aboard two US Navy warships stationed in the South China Sea, USS *Galveston* and USS *Wichita*, used to stage mock musical battles on the open seas using his songs. As it awaited refuelling, the *Galveston* would play 'Galveston' over its PA to the approaching *Wichita*, which responded by blasting 'Wichita Lineman'. (Four decades later, R.E.M. would release a response song called 'Houston'.)

More importantly, because 'By the Time I Get to Phoenix', 'Wichita Lineman', 'Galveston' and 'Where's the Playground, Susie?' (another Jimmy Webb classic that was released in April 1969 as the second single from the *Galveston* album, and again written about Susan Horton)

193

were such massive hits, they redefined what a pop single could be: complex emotions and idiosyncratic arrangements and orchestrations, coupled with Campbell-like no-frills delivery and emotional purity.

'Galveston' certainly helped Campbell's upward trajectory. In the summer of 1968, in the wake of his success with 'Phoenix' and 'Wichita', he guest-hosted *The Smothers Brothers Comedy Hour*. The successful appearance led to his own variety show, *The Glen Campbell Goodtime Hour*, which ran until 1972. The likes of Ray Charles, Johnny Cash and Linda Ronstadt appeared on the programme, which also gave a national platform to rising country stars like Willie Nelson. 'He exposed us to a big part of the world that would have never had the chance to see us,' said Nelson. Having become a proper TV star, Campbell built himself a gargantuan 16,500-square-foot house on a hill high up in Laurel Canyon.

A young Steve Martin was a writer on the show. 'He just went along with it,' says Martin. 'He was completely game, and completely fun, and had kind of a down-home sense of humour. It was just an incredible treat for us young writers to be introduced to talent at that level at such a young age.'

Campbell looked like a cowboy, so much so that he was cast opposite John Wayne in the ageing hero's 1969 vehicle *True Grit*. Campbell was blond as the midday sun, solid as a hay bale and with a seemingly never-ending supply of hats, embroidered denim, western shirts and cowboy boots. He later said that his acting was so amateurish that he 'gave

John Wayne that push to win the Academy Award'. Wayne didn't appear to be too enamoured of his co-star, however, and gave him the same advice he gave Michael Caine when he first came to Hollywood: 'Kid, talk low, talk slow, and don't say too much. Then you'll be fine.' Campbell's first starring vehicle, *Norwood*, flopped, however, and the hits dried up until he bounced back into town with the studied countrypolitan pop of 'Rhinestone Cowboy' in 1975. 'Cowboy' had already been turned down by both Elvis and Neil Diamond by the time it was offered to Campbell. A reflective piece about pursuing the American Dream, it immediately became one of Campbell's signature tunes. According to its author, Larry Weiss, the chorus came from the 1944 movie *Buffalo Bill*, in the last scene of which Bill rides out on a white horse, in a white outfit and with a long white beard, and thanks everybody for giving him such a great life.

There would be more country albums, too, as Campbell attempted to reconnect with a constituency he had always been in two minds about. He tried what a lot of crossover artists had done before, and would do again, namely get more country – very country. Dolly Parton had done the same thing: after all the fame, the smash records and the hit movies – there was a time when you couldn't turn on the radio without hearing 'Jolene' or '9 to 5' – the country girl moved away from commercial music and successfully reconnected with the genre she grew up with – bluegrass. 'If I could have made a living, and still had the career, doing this kind of music, I would have done that,' she said. 'I had to get rich in order to afford to sing like I was poor again. Isn't that a hell of a note?'

Campbell would marry four times, producing five sons and three daughters (some of whom would eventually play with him on stage, which contributed to much sibling rivalry between the various families). In 1980, after his third divorce, he said, 'Perhaps I've found the secret for an unhappy private life. Every three years I go and marry a girl who doesn't love me, and then she proceeds to take all my money.' That year, he started a short, tempestuous and very high-profile relationship with the singer Tanya Tucker, who was twenty-three years his junior. At the time, he was battling alcoholism and cocaine addiction, so the affair made him tabloid catnip. He showered her with jewels, spent nearly $60,000 on her birthday party and at one point was going to underwrite a high-fashion boutique, Rhinestone Cowgirl, that she was planning to open in Beverly Hills. In his heyday Campbell had been saddled with nicknames such as the 'Farmboy Choirboy' and the 'Hip Hick', but his dalliance with Tucker soon put paid to those. She had exploded into the country charts at the age of thirteen with 'Delta Dawn', rapidly racking up half a dozen other hits while posing in black leather and tight skimpy tops. Overnight she became the wild child of country and western. When they started seeing each other – she only twenty-one and he a forty-four-year-old grandfather – she boasted, 'He's the horniest man I ever met. Men are supposed to slow down after forty, but it's just the opposite with Glen. I mean, I thought I could handle a lot.' The relationship faltered, apparently because of Campbell's jealousy, although their behaviour seemed to be aggravated by a relationship with booze and cocaine that could apparently be called 'attentive'. ('He did cocaine more than just about anybody,' said his friend Alice Cooper.) After they split, Tucker would file a $3 million lawsuit against her former lover, charging 'Battery, Mayhem, Assault with a deadly weapon, and Fraud'. The case was settled out of court, although never again would Campbell be called the Farmboy Choirboy. Because if, with his voice, he had once been able to weaponise sadness, with this kind of tabloid behaviour all he had managed to do was encourage pity. In 1981, for instance, he became embroiled in such a heated argument with a member of the Indonesian government on a long-haul flight that he promised to 'call my friend Ronald Reagan and ask him to bomb Jakarta'.

After his years of substance abuse, it perhaps wasn't any great surprise that Campbell would eventually find religion – obviously such a well-worn stepping stone on the Nashville path to redemption – and because of this he developed some particularly unsavoury opinions, notably involving the pro-life movement. And then in 1982 he married Kimberly Woollen, a Radio City Music Hall Rockette, who helped Campbell get sober.

'On our first date he took me to a restaurant at the Waldorf and before we ate he bowed his head and said a prayer and I thought, "Oh good, he believes in God,"' she said. 'Of course, as the night went on I also found out he had an alcohol problem. But he [was] always such a great person; so generous, so sweet and loving and kind. It was just the alcohol that turned him into a monster. He was obnoxious. He was mean. It wasn't the Glen I knew him to be. So we got involved in the church and started studying the Bible together and got some godly friends around who encouraged you. We started surrounding ourselves with family. His brother came to live with us and Shorty said, "Glen, I don't want you to end up like Elvis, you really need to stop drinking." Gene Autry called him and said, "The booze is no good, Glen." So a lot of people who loved him encouraged him. He would fall down drunk five nights a week. Just pass out. I would never advise anybody to do what I did; go into a relationship knowing that someone is so messed up.'

Jimmy Webb also witnessed Campbell's bizarre duality. 'With Glen, there used to be something definitely disconcerting about the mix between the Holy Bible and the cocaine. He would be delivering the most astounding lecture from the Old Testament, and at the same time there would be lines laid out on the table. It was just surreal.'

In 2003, Campbell fell off the wagon in spectacular fashion and was arrested for a hit-and-run, pleading guilty to extreme drunken driving and leaving the scene of an accident, and spending ten days in jail. Robert Chalmers interviewed him for the *Independent on Sunday* in 2007, in the

Orleans Casino in Las Vegas, and enjoyed the way in which the singer could talk about his misdemeanours without rancour. He was in a happy place and could largely laugh at some of the scrapes he'd been in. Largely. 'If there's a drawback to frequenting a public area such as this, it's that many of the looks he does attract are connected not so much with his artistic output, as with his arrest for driving while intoxicated near Phoenix, Arizona, in November 2003,' wrote Chalmers. 'The police photograph – to his great distress – has become the most famous single image of Campbell: wide-eyed and handcuffed wearing a reversed baseball cap, Arizona Diamondbacks T-shirt, shorts and trainers. The picture was taken after his silver BMW performed a bold and unorthodox manoeuvre, resulting in a collision with a vehicle driven by a sommelier called Mr Roote.' Campbell compounded his crime by kneeing the police officer in the thigh while resisting arrest. The officer said he smelled alcohol on Campbell's breath, and when he knocked on his car door, the singer kneed him in the leg, landing himself an aggravated assault charge. After pleading guilty he was sentenced to ten days in prison, but when he was questioned about it later, he said, 'I wasn't really that drunk. I was just over-served.'

Eventually he got clean. Eight years later, the *Guardian*'s Simon Hattenstone went to LA to interview him, offering a vignette of the Campbells' churchly domesticity: 'We are sitting in a large sunlit villa looking over the Malibu hills and surrounded by memorabilia from Campbell's career. There are trophy cabinets and rooms full of photographs of

Campbell with Elvis, Dean Martin, Ray Charles and Sammy
Davis Jr and everybody who was everybody – permanent
reminders of who he was. Huge leather-bound Bibles, far
too heavy to pick up, lie on tables. Kim was brought up
in the Methodist Presbyterian church, he in the Church of
Christ, Baptist, but early into their marriage they joined a
Messianic synagogue that follows the Old Testament but
believes Jesus is the Messiah. The Campbells eat kosher
and celebrate Jewish festivals. On Friday nights, Campbell
blesses the bread and wine.'

'God saved me,' he told Hattenstone.

The abuse never seemed to affect his voice, though. It
was always sweet, but never too sweet, even when he was
singing dentist music. 'He had the pure flowing tone of
a crooner but with something smoky in there, a whiskey
catch at the back of his throat that tugged at the heart of
a melody and left listeners feeling every shift in the lyric,'
wrote Neil McCormick in an obituary of Campbell in the
Irish Independent. 'He had an impossible range that could
pluck notes out of the ether but somehow made every song
he ever sang sound easy.' Obits tend to go one of two ways,
either by using inordinate amounts of flattery or by dimin-
ishing achievement. McCormick was fulsome in his praise,
meaning every word of it. 'His readings of Webb's country
gothic classics surely stand amongst the greatest records
ever made,' he wrote. Webb once told him it was easy to
write his vastly ambitious, deeply romantic songs knowing
he had Campbell to sing them.

McCormick also mentioned one of the reasons why Campbell was such a great interpreter of Webb's material, something that had actually been acknowledged by both of them: namely that he always seemed a little bit out of time himself. Campbell sat between two stools, between country and pop, between the swing era and rock and roll, between old-fashioned values and new-fashioned attitudes. He was in his own vortex, in a cultural never-never land. McCormick describes watching him on his Saturday-night TV show, handsome and wholesome, yet with an edge that came, perhaps, from his country roots. 'There were subtle dimensions of doubt and pain that resonated in his rich chord changes and lush orchestrations, the inescapable sense there was more going on than met the eye.' He was, as he sang himself, a rhinestone cowboy.

'He had that beautiful tenor with a crystal-clear guitar sound, playing lines that were so inventive,' said Tom Petty in 2011. 'It moved me.'

Campbell was always very respectful of Jimmy Webb, and more than grateful that he had benefited so much from his partner's ability to write songs that helped define him as an entertainer. There are dozens of old clips of Campbell appearing on TV chat shows, willingly sitting down in the comfy chair opposite the likes of Johnny Carson or Craig Kilborn, often with a guitar in his hand, and always with a big smile on his face. The singer always took his success seriously, never took it for granted, and understood that the people who bought his records and turned up at his concerts could just as easily change their minds and start spending their money on someone else. So, for him, appearing on one of those chat shows wasn't a chore or an inconvenience, it was all part of the show, all part of the entertainer's life. And wasn't he lucky to have one?

As he sinks into the chair, you can often detect a nervous glance at the host, which is when you can see Campbell's carapace crack for a moment, as he looks across and wonders what the smart-ass TV men were going to say to him, instinctively worrying that they were going to make some gag or other. But even when they did – and it usually seemed to be affectionate – he'd flip whatever it was right back at them, his all-enveloping smile getting bigger as he did so. He'd try and keep the conversation light, remind everyone how lucky he was, what fun he was having, and how he was sure that their lives would be improved no end by buying into whatever he was on the show to push.

He would often be asked about his relationship with Jimmy Webb, and then the smile would be put away. When discussing his friend, Campbell would be even more respectful than he was about his own career, paying homage to a man he would repeatedly call a genius, a man who conjured such beautiful songs. Occasionally he would become proprietorial, in a way that a football manager might be about a player, where the emphasis on the relationship inevitably infers that one works for the other, although even when the singer hinted that the songwriter was a hired hand, he made sure that everyone knew his hands were the finest in the business. Glen Campbell loved Jimmy Webb. He had his back.

'Webb's stuff is a little bit country. But . . . actually I don't like to segregate music,' said Campbell. 'To me it's like segregating people . . . People who say, "That's Country and I don't like Country" gotta be pretty narrow-minded. Either that or they don't know a damn thing about music. "I don't like country music" – that's the dumbest remark I ever heard. Then you start naming off some country songs and they say, "Is that Country? I didn't know that." There's good in all music. It's like when I record, I don't aim at anything. I just find a good song and go do it like I want to. And if the country fans gripe or the pop fans gripe, I can't help it.'

In 2006, when Campbell was in his seventies, he said that he still sang 'Wichita Lineman' with genuine emotion. 'I think it's as good a chord progression and melody as I've ever seen. I'm so glad that I had hits with songs that I like,' he said, 'because I know a lot of guys who say, "If I have to sing that song one more time I'm getting out of the business." That's so stupid.'

It's easy to spot those entertainers who begrudge performing their earlier, more successful work, perhaps the songs that made them famous. They'll look upon them as sketches, bagatelles, mere crumbs that pale in comparison to the bigger, grander, more mature work they're performing now, in spite of the fact that neither the critics nor the public appear to be taking much interest in it. Glen Campbell never felt this way, and he was more than happy to play

'Wichita Lineman' or 'By the Time I Get to Phoenix' if that was what the TV producer wanted. It would be great if he could play one from the new album as well, yet he understood that he had a sturdy and popular enough back catalogue to satisfy demand.

Like Burt Bacharach, another composer who wanted to sing, Jimmy Webb didn't want to be just the architect, he wanted to be the building, too; and while, in the early seventies, he was starting to work with some of the finest vocalists in the business, Webb insisted on interpreting his songs himself. His voice, as someone once put it, couldn't always call on the colours his challenging material required, and yet he was determined to make it as a solo performer.

Webb had an all-access pass to those at both ends of the culture, working with Sinatra in Vegas one minute and Joni Mitchell in Laurel Canyon the next. Increasingly popular with the mainstream, he was nevertheless smitten by the new breed of singer-songwriters, people like Mitchell, James Taylor, Randy Newman and Jackson Browne. 'What they were doing was almost conversational. People like Joni were fishing beneath the thermal clime, and so I began to reach very deep into the soul for my songs.' He wasn't always welcomed with open arms, though. He came into the studio one night when Mitchell was recording, and a voice behind him said, 'Oh, it's Mr Balloons.' For a lot of people, Webb's songs felt too conservative, too showbiz. 'They felt packaged for a middle-of-the-road, older crowd,' said Tom Petty. 'At first, you go, "Oh, I don't know about that." But it was such pure, good stuff that you had to put off your prejudices and learn to love it. It taught me not to have those prejudices.'

Apart from Harry Nilsson (who was as much of a drinking buddy as anything else), the singer/songwriter he was closest to was Mitchell. 'She sang backgrounds on my albums – was a joy to be around – and was a great teacher because she's really one of the finest song constructors that's ever lived. And very open, she wasn't biased, she wasn't like, "Oh, this guy writes songs for Glen Campbell, I can't hang out with him." People in the early seventies were *extremely* sensitive to what was politically correct. To the point of bigotry. As guilty of bigotry as any group of people who've ever lived.'

To some, he epitomised mainstream culture, and not in a good way. He was one of those named in Gil Scott-Heron's 'The Revolution Will Not Be Televised', in which Scott-Heron says that the theme song won't be sung by Glen Campbell, Tom Jones, Johnny Cash, Engelbert Humperdinck or the Rare Earth, nor written by Webb.

Webb certainly adopted the lifestyle of a rock star, and having acquired the Encino estate of former screen goddess Alice Faye, blew his considerable wealth on cocaine and cars, crashing a Shelby 427 Cobra five times and raising hell with the likes of Harry Nilsson.

The eighteen-month period between early 1968 and late 1969 was an extraordinary one for Webb, when his entire being was reimagined, and when he went from being a Nobody to a Somebody. After the success of 'Up, Up and Away', 'By the Time I Get to Phoenix' and 'Wichita Lineman', he was afforded so many opportunities, some of which he grabbed and some of which he squandered (he still regrets not returning a call from Paul McCartney in the summer of 1968). However, in 1969, he managed to find the time to produce Thelma Houston's debut album, *Sunshower*. Unsuccessful at the time – it reached no. 50 on the *Billboard* R&B charts – it has since become recognised as something of a lost classic. Made by the former lead vocalist of a group called the Art Reynolds Singers, much was expected of the record. Webb was hot, she was new, and Dunhill Records thought the stars, and the public, would look kindly on the collaboration. It was not to be. One reviewer said the album was one of those perfect records that let the singer and producer complement one another without either stealing the show. But the public weren't interested.

In 1970, Webb talked briefly to David Geffen about being managed by him, but Geffen, the playmakers' playmaker, could see this wouldn't be an easy gig. Like everyone else in the industry, he could see that Webb was caught between two stools, frozen between two buses going in different directions – one going uptown to where all the fancy supper-club people went, the other moving downtown, where supper club meant something else entirely. Webb explained to Geffen that he had turned down a ton of money to play a residency in Vegas (performing an instrumental version of 'MacArthur Park' every night, in costume, in front of a full orchestra), told him his favourite singer was Joni Mitchell, told him he probably smoked more grass than everyone else Geffen managed, combined. But even with Geffen's help, Webb was stranded, neither fish nor fowl.

As he told Robert Hilburn of the *Los Angeles Times* in 1971, 'By the time I was twenty-one, I had accomplished all the goals I had set up for myself for a lifetime. That's destructive in a way. You have all this energy left and you don't know exactly what to do with it. You find yourself sitting down and saying: "Well, that's fine for today; now, what am I going to do tomorrow?" From what I've seen of this business, there is a tendency for songwriters, once they have become successful, to stick to a formula. They drift along in the formula that established them, playing the same kind of songs until they die, I suppose. Maybe I'll learn in my lifetime that it has to be that way, but I hope it isn't true.

'I decided that I wanted to keep writing, that I wanted to evolve. I wanted to break out of the formula. I wanted to improve as a writer and to interpret the songs myself rather than just keep producing records and writing songs for other artists.'

But the songs kept coming, exquisite little gems such as 'P. F. Sloan', 'One Lady', 'Met Her on a Plane', 'When Can Brown Begin?', 'Crying in My Sleep', 'Scissors Cut', 'Christiaan, No', 'Gauguin', 'Skywriter', 'Time Flies', etc. – songs that showed real depth, real meaning, songs delivered with plenty of grace and a minimum of fuss. Everything Webb did in the early seventies was designed to single him out as a performer as much as a writer, everything a defiant act of self-ownership.

'I made my share of mistakes, probably more than my share, but I gained an understanding of what fame was like,' he told me. 'I had way too much money for a twenty-year-old kid, let me tell you. I also became acquainted with the phenomenon of when you are a celebrity, you're always right. There's always a group of willing participants, of enablers. You drive by a dealership in Beverly Hills and you see a beautiful sedan and you remark to your assistant, "Wow, I'd really like to have one of those, that's nice," and then the next morning it's sitting in your driveway – that kind of stuff. For a while I was convinced that I could write a hit any time I wanted to. And an experience like the "Wichita Lineman" story will make you think that that's actually true. Then you start coming up against it and you realise it isn't that easy, and that all is not what it seems. I can remember sitting at a fancy dinner with a radio-programme director back in the Midwest somewhere, maybe Chicago. I'm sitting there and I'm talking, being cordial, and the programme director's wife put her hands down in her lap, as women do, and she looked at me as though to say enough of this nonsense, and said, "So, when are you going to write a 'MacArthur Park'?" And I realised that what she meant was, when was I going to write another hit?'

In 1973, he would overdose on PCP – 'enough to kill an elephant' – having taken it believing it was cocaine, and temporarily lose his ability to play the piano. Like Glen

Campbell, he would later eschew drugs, although without exchanging them for God. His final seventies album, *El Mirage*, was produced in LA by George Martin, but despite containing such orch-pop nuggets as 'The Highwayman', 'Where the Universes Are' and 'The Moon Is a Harsh Mistress', its commercial failure was something of a blow to Webb, who didn't release another record for five years. He would continue collaborating with Campbell, though, continue having hits. In 1975, they collaborated on 'It's a Sin When You Love Somebody', and in 1987 developed another classic song, 'Still Within the Sound of My Voice', written by Webb and sung by Campbell, which reached no. 5 on the *Billboard* Country charts. It was covered brilliantly by Linda Ronstadt two years later.

So where did they come from, these words, these conflicts and trials, these battle-weary vignettes and musical pictures? Where do they come from now? Webb wrote an entire book about songwriting (and a very brilliant one at that, maybe the very best – *Tunesmith: Inside the Art of Songwriting* (1999)), and when pushed will admit to getting his ideas from the same place every other songwriter does, from anywhere and everywhere, using his own particular brand of symbolism and spiritualism. He tells a fascinating story about the inspiration for his song 'The Highwayman'.

He'd been staying at the Inn on the Park in London, 'hanging out with Harry Nilsson and behaving badly. And I had this room with a piano in it and one night I had this Dick Turpinesque nightmare about being chased by these grenadiers on horseback. And I was fairly certain if they caught me they'd hang me. It was one of those night terrors where the sheets are soaked. And I woke up and I could *feel* this character. I could see him and feel him and I rolled out of bed to the piano and in an hour I had the first verse. The idea was that he'd been caught and hung and then I decided to drop him into another body.'

'And this magical lyric about reincarnation rolls out that seems to span four hundred years,' said Mark Ellen, who thinks it's one of the greatest lyrics ever written. 'It starts in the eighteenth century with the image of the highway-man with his sword and pistol relieving young maidens of their baubles. He's killed and reborn as a sailor in the nine-teenth century aboard a schooner (Webb once told me he was writing about "the age of the clipper ships", which was around 1850). And he's drowned in an accident and gets reborn as a dam-builder in the twentieth century, who dies when he falls into the wet concrete of the Hoover Dam. And the dam-builder's reborn in a distant twenty-first-century future as a space pilot flying "a starship across the universe divide". And the pilot may return as a high-wayman, so the whole four-century jumble of creation is about to reboot. Or, he adds as an afterthought, he may return "as a single drop of rain", the most powerful and head-spinning lyric about space and time I've ever heard. I can't think of another song as huge and encompassing. And it's circular, so it seems eternal. It has an immaculate, giddying symmetry, so much compressed into so few lines, and all carried by a gorgeous melody. It's a masterpiece. It's perfect.'

Webb is justly proud of 'Wichita Lineman' and has often said that it's his own favourite, and praises its perfection (seen through a prism of imperfections, obviously). However, he has also been exasperated by its seemingly random popularity.

'I'm just telling you from a songwriter's point of view that sometimes I am absolutely amazed at the take someone will have for one song and how oblivious they are to another one that I've laboured over and burnt the midnight oil over and suffered over, and it goes by with no notice whatsoever,' he said, not with any anger but with something approaching incredulity. 'I'm somewhat bewildered by it. I would like to be as grateful as I could possibly be. It's just another song to me. I've written a thousand of them, and it's really just another one.'

Supportive of his friend as ever, Campbell was convinced Webb's songs would last for ever, confident enough to proclaim that they were as good as anything that had been written, that would be written. Campbell grew up in an age when some songs were deemed to be standards, and he was sure enough of his own opinion and such a devotee of the work that he knew these songs would stand the test of time. Because they were modern standards, that's why.

'I don't think of me as a country writer,' Webb told GQ's Jason Barlow, 'but Glen cherished me as a writer. There was no way in the world he was going to say anything to alienate me enough where I'd say to him, "Fuck you and your cow-boy shit!!" And I'd go off and write songs for Bette Midler, or something.'

Webb is the only artist ever to have received Grammy Awards for music, lyrics and orchestration. He's been given the Ivor Novello International Award and the Academy of Country Music's Poet Award, and was the youngest person ever inducted into the Songwriters Hall of Fame. In May 2012, at the Ivor Novello Awards in London, he received the songwriting equivalent of an endorsement from the Almighty. As he was presented with the Special International Award, a vintage quote flashed on the screen, in which Sammy Cahn, the legendary lyricist and con-tributor to the Great American Songbook, the co-writer of dozens of timeless ballads such as 'Three Coins in the Fountain', 'Come Fly with Me', 'All the Way', 'Call Me Irresponsible' and 'My Kind of Town', described Webb as 'one of the real, real geniuses'. Increasingly inclined to call himself a romanticist, Webb continued to use the kind of vivid imagery his contemporaries had long abandoned. 'I like words,' he said. 'I like the way they clash around together and bang up against each other, especially in songs.'

John Updike had a famous line about trying to give 'the mundane its beautiful due' in his writing, and you could say that Webb has devoted a large part of his songwriting career to doing precisely that. 'My style is novelistic, detailed,' he said. 'I draw the audience into my problem or my world and hope that they feel like "I've felt that before, I just didn't know how to say it." A songwriter's job is to articulate these feelings. When you do that well, then quite often you find out you have a hit song.'

Mark Ellen once asked Webb why so many songwriters are drawn to melancholic songs. 'Well, there's a lot of happy songs, but they're not very good. You can dash off four in an afternoon. The territory I tend to inhabit is that sort of "crushed lonely hearts" thing. The first part of a relationship is usually that white-hot centre when all the happy songs come. When that's gone it can be devastating, and that's when the sorrowful songs come.'

Webb continues to be an influence on modern writers, and you only have to study the reviews of the Arctic Monkeys' *Tranquility Base Hotel & Casino* to see that some think Webb has made as much of an impact on Alex Turner's writing as David Bowie. It's also rare to read anything about Josh Tillman or his alter ego Father John Misty without seeing a reference to Webb or Glen Campbell.

The one missed opportunity in Webb's career was the chance to record with Elvis, although it wasn't for lack of trying. 'It was certainly nothing that I did that prevented me from working with him,' Webb said, pointing the blame squarely at Elvis's notoriously controlling manager Colonel Tom Parker. 'I have bootleg recordings of Elvis doing "MacArthur Park" and "By the Time I Get to Phoenix". We talked about recording together, but Colonel Tom Parker insisted on one hundred per cent of the publishing. I was being recorded by Mr Sinatra and Tony Bennett and Glen

Campbell and I just didn't feel that I was in a position where I had to make that kind of a sacrifice. In retrospect I would have loved to have had a record with him, but I guess I stood on principle and it wouldn't be the first time or the last time in life that I would cut off my nose to spite my face.'

If you study Elvis's records from the late sixties onwards, after he'd finally finished with the movies, they are all strikingly similar – maudlin, melodramatic, almost as if everything in life was something of a fait accompli. You can almost hear him shrugging his shoulders, giving up, feeling blue for you, on stage, on record, where everyone can see and hear. There would be the occasional tacky rocker, a schmaltzy R&B number that would allow him to swing his hips again and 'rock out' a little, but the bulk of his material was sad and fatalistic.

Webb was fascinated by Elvis's work, and not just the early stuff. 'I listened to Elvis Presley a lot,' he said. 'And as a teenager, I was enchanted and hypnotized by Burt Bacharach and Hal David's songs, so I followed them and what they did with Dionne Warwick. I listened to Tony Hatch and, also, to Teddy Randazzo, who wrote "Hurt So Bad" and "Goin' Out of My Head" for Little Anthony. That was always the thing for me – the big orchestral ballad – my weak spot. So I would imitate those guys when I could and I always had dreams of using an orchestra on my records. And as fate would have it, I was able to do that. I was eventually able to teach myself orchestration on the job, so to speak.'

He also saw Elvis perform his first-ever show in Vegas, in what would become the King's natural habitat. 'Vegas was great for all of us, because you could get up close to the animal. You know, you could practically get Sinatra's sweat on you. It was very visceral. You should have seen the kind of money that was changing hands, just to get closer to the stage. Anything to get closer to the stage. I saw Elvis when he came back and opened at the International Hotel [what became the Hilton International]. A lot of people from LA went up, thinking no one really knew what Elvis was gonna do, as it had been a long time since he had played a live show. Even Elvis didn't know what was going to happen. He was very nervous about it. I think a lot of cynics went up, kind of hoping, "Yeah, I hope he falls on his ass . . .", that kind of thing. I kind of went up dispassionately, you know, thinking I just want to check this out. I walked into this gorgeous showroom, brand new, probably two thousand people. I think they served two thousand dinners at each performance. That first night, I was sitting right next to the stage, and about six seats down this guy was glowering at me, giving me a bad face. I was closer than anyone. But Elvis came out and did the whole Elvis thing, and I just became an Elvis fan to the core. There was no doubting that there was this magic, a magnetism that just permeated the room, just got inside you. James Burton playing guitar, great drumming, he was very solid in the rhythm section and he knew what he was doing there. And he was a rocker, he really was the king of rock and roll. After the show he walked right down to the front of the stage and was giving out silk scarves to all the girls, as by now there were hundreds of girls around the stage, and he was kissing them. He gets down on the stage, bends over me, and I'm thinking, "Oh, God, he's going to kiss me." I had really long hair at the time. But he dropped a note, a piece of paper on the table, and the note said, "Jimmy, come back stage. Elvis." And after the show these two burly highway patrol-type guys half carried me through the crowd, back through the kitchen and through all these double doors, and finally came up to this drab-looking dressing room, and they pushed open the door and Colonel Tom Parker was there . . .'

And that was that.

In the same way that Parker didn't entertain the idea of missing out on any royalties, so Elvis never really understood the concept of 'the album'. As pop began to expand in the mid-sixties, and as concept albums became commonplace, Elvis stuck to the time-honoured formula of an album being a portmanteau collection of singles, bits and pieces and not much else. His albums were all filler, no killer. Elvis was never going to be interested in making anything like *Sgt. Pepper* or *Wish You Were Here*, but he also had no interest in producing a modern echo of *Songs for Swinging Lovers*, the Frank Sinatra LP that is often credited with being the first concept album. Elvis could be an exemplary interpreter of popular song, and when he chose the right one, he'd find it relatively easy to turn it into a classic, or turn in a version that made people say he 'owned it'. But, absurdly, he couldn't knit together a dozen of them, had no interest in running alongside Simon & Garfunkel or Todd Rundgren, or even keeping up with Fleetwood Mac or Neil Diamond, a man who probably wouldn't have had a career were it not for Elvis. He was such an influential figure that he could have commanded the very best songwriters in the world to pitch him songs. Would Lennon and McCartney have turned down an opportunity to write an entire album for Elvis? Would Dylan? Would Jimmy Webb? Towards the end of the sixties, Lennon and McCartney's relationship was in such a parlous state that writing to order might have encouraged them to be more collaborative. Also, even though Elvis had long been diminished in their eyes by a decade of poor product, neither of them could ever forget the debt they owed him, would never forget the debt the entire industry owed him, and they would have looked upon the project as an honour. At the time, they were thinking about the past a lot, and having tired of the convoluted way they had been recording for the last three or four years, were looking forward to recording live again, feeling like a band again and focusing on simpler material. When they initially started recording *Let It Be*, they would break into old rock and roll classics in between their new songs, bashing away at 'Stand by Me', 'Blue Suede Shoes', 'Words of Love' and 'Save the Last Dance for Me'. Imagine if a relationship with Elvis had been formed, and imagine him singing some of the more spartan material Lennon would go on to record for the *Plastic Ono Band* LP . . . Imagine, for instance,

Elvis singing 'Working Class Hero'. Imagine Elvis hearing a demo of 'Let It Be' and deciding that he had to record it before anyone else, including the man who wrote it. But of course he was never going to hear the demo because he never socialised, never travelled, and kept himself to himself, living out Groundhog Day at Graceland. Elvis wasn't going to a cocktail party, Elvis wasn't hanging out at the wrap party for *Easy Rider*, wasn't going to the Oscars, wasn't going to appear on *The Tonight Show*, wasn't going anywhere outside Memphis, not if he could help it.

'He loved "MacArthur Park",' Webb said of Presley. 'I don't say that to brag. It's been documented. I have a tape of him singing it. At that time, though, I wanted to get a song done by Elvis. But as I was leaving after my meeting with Elvis, Col. Parker followed me to the door and said, "I guess we won't be seeing you here again." I said, "Oh, really?"' Parker wanted only songs to which he could get full publishing rights, and as Webb says, 'I didn't need Elvis to record "MacArthur Park". It was already a number one hit. Col. Parker was a crude man . . . He was the man who told Elvis he shouldn't record with the Beatles.'

The closest that Webb came to a collaboration with Elvis was making him the subject of his 1991 song 'Elvis and Me', based on his various meetings with him.*

---

* Glen Campbell befriended Presley when he helped record the soundtrack for *Viva Las Vegas* in 1964. He later said, 'Elvis and I were brought up the same humble way – picking cotton and looking at the north end of a south-bound mule.' Campbell was a terrific mimic, and one of his best impressions was Elvis singing 'That's Alright (Mama)'.

One night in early 1976 they were on stage together in Las Vegas. 'It was just incredible,' said Campbell. 'In Vegas, I was kidding him. He introduced me and said, "Campbell, I understand you're doing an imitation of me. I just want you to know it will always be an imitation." And I said, "I'm not gonna do it no more. I got to gain some weight first." He laughed, and the audience went, "Oh, hey, boo." I said, "Can't you take a joke?" Elvis could take it, but the audience just got on my ass. Elvis said, "Well, when you're down here next I'm coming down and I'm gonna sit in the front row and read a newspaper and heckle." The audience laughed, and I said, "Elvis, if I'm singing as good as you are, I won't care." Backstage we were talking, and I said, "Did you believe the way the people reacted?" Elvis said, "Yeah, I know, it's like everything is supposedly taboo because people are afraid they will say something that isn't true." He didn't say lied, he said tell you something other than the facts. That makes life so much harder to deal with than if people tell you what they think. People are afraid to say, "Hey, Elvis, you're fat." I didn't say, Hey Elvis you're fat, I just said you better back away from the table. I mean there are cool ways of handling it. In fact, I was teasing and said can I have some of your old clothes. He said, "Campbell, you ain't getting 'em. I'm gonna grow back into them."'

Their mutual respect was huge. Elvis would cover Campbell's 'Gentle on My Mind' during his *From Elvis in Memphis* sessions with producer Chips Moman in 1969, while a year later Presley suggested Campbell recut Conway Twitty's fifties hit 'It's Only Make Believe', which he did, yielding a massive worldwide hit. Both Campbell and Presley would become top draws playing Las Vegas in the late sixties, often seeing each other perform. As Campbell would recall, 'When we played . . . in Vegas, [Elvis] would go in for a month, and I'd go in for a month. Then we'd switch. Elvis had more charisma in his little finger than everybody else put together. What d'you call it? Electricity.'

7: COUNTY MUSIC

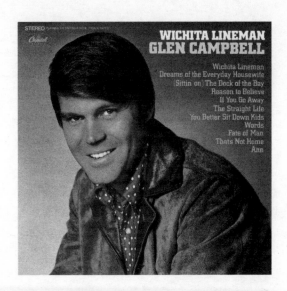

> At the CMAs [the Country Music
> Awards], I performed with Little
> Big Town and we just did this
> transcendent version of 'Wichita
> Lineman', which they've been
> doing all summer on their tour . . .
> It keeps me young to be around
> this new generation. I learn things
> about what's going on. It's a
> conduit to the real world.

JIMMY WEBB

In 2018, 'Wichita Lineman' was on the set list for the concert tours of Toby Keith, Little Big Town and Guns N' Roses. In the fifty years since it was released, hundreds of boldface names have come out of the closet and expressed their admiration for the song. It seems an entire generation had been harbouring deep love for Jimmy Webb's greatest creation ever since it was released. Acknowledging this was almost as important as feeling it. In October 2006, the Rolling Stones played Wichita for the first and presumably last time. 'We are the virgins of Wichita,' said Mick Jagger from the stage, before strapping on an acoustic guitar and treating the crowd to the first verse of 'Wichita Lineman'. Jagger smiled. 'I bet everyone who comes here does that.'

Rolling Stone would rank it the sixteenth greatest country song of all time ('The sound – a haze of soapy violins and expensive chord changes – had more to do with the onset of soft rock than the rudiments of country, but the subject matter was a new spin on an old story. Country calls it individualism; Webb called it loneliness'); *Time Out* ranked it the twenty-ninth greatest country song of all time; the *NME* said it was one of the best twenty-five country songs of all time; while *Pitchfork* understandably listed it as one of the two hundred best songs of the sixties.

Webb would never write a third verse, claiming that would have been gilding the lily. Part of the charm of it, for the writer, was that it was minimalist. Not only is it unfinished, he said, it also contains a false rhyme ('time' and 'line'), something that Webb says he didn't notice until years after he'd written it.

'What is incredible to me is that I never heard it before, and then all of a sudden I did!' he told me. '"I need you more than want you / and I want you for all time / And the Wichita lineman is still on the line." Those consonants are different, that's a false rhyme. Which doesn't mean much in pop music, to tell you the truth, as people by and large don't pay any attention to them. But the true lyricists – the Oscar Hammersteins, the Lorenz Harts, the Cole Porters, those guys – they were pretty fastidious about this kind of stuff. However, I think that "Wichita Lineman" might be one of those cases where it's probably worth it.'

When we eventually met, Webb also admitted to another mistake in the song, one I wasn't aware of.

'I might as well tell you, because someone is going to want to talk to you about it. I made technical errors when I wrote the song. I had two different kinds of power lines on my telephone pole. I talk about an overload, which is something that happens to high-tension wires, but I cast the main character as a telephone repair man, fixing the line.'

Getting his wires crossed, literally.

'Some of the guys from the union have scolded me about that from time to time, but it's very hard to explain poetic licence to a union member . . .'

Andrew Collins, the journalist and former editor of *Q*, has written extensively about the song. 'It feels like a story and yet, broken down, the lyric is quite spare. But it's not a poem, and Webb's not just a wordsmith. Glen Campbell brings the song to heartbroken life and a country authenticity to the sound pictures. His vocal is coffee-smooth – perhaps sipped from a flask – and conveys the plaintive in our lineman's lament for lost love in such a sincere and moving way you could never see him as a telegraphic stalker. He means it, man. And the held note at the end of "still on the *liiiiiiiine*" seems to echo around the wide-open plains, as if the shot is panning back, wider and wider, until he's a speck on a stick.

'The string arrangement does some daring wire work, too. After a descending guitar twang and patted intro beat, there they swirl, filling the Kansas sky with sun, while violins and a keyboard get to work on the pre-digital approximation of a telegraph's bleeps and whines. Invention permeates.

'It's a downhome, nice-and-simple, over-easy slice of life which finds symbolism in the horny hands of the working man and creates something almost space-age out of its allotted instruments. And it's sung by Campbell like it *matters*. My friend Stuart Maconie called it the "greatest pop song ever composed", and I think his tribute is contained in the word "composed". "Wichita Lineman" doesn't feel written, or knocked out to order, it's a novella that's been inspired by real life and if it's a little bit country, it feels more local than that.

'It's *county* music.'

'I first heard the song when I was about six or seven, on pop radio, although I really got to know it when my dad bizarrely bought an album called *Glen Campbell's Greatest Hits*, which wasn't actually by Glen Campbell,' said Stuart Maconie. 'It was one of those cheap *Top of the Pops* records where the songs are actually recorded by other people, but even then I knew that "Wichita Lineman" was something special. Here you have this man with an inexplicable inner life, an unfathomable, unnamed man who has this extraordinary inner life. He has this Raymond Carver, Richard Ford, Harold Pinter aura about him, as does the song. Less is more. In some ways the song's incompleteness is its salvation, as it's actually quite thin, allowing us as listeners to fill in the rest. How Jimmy Webb managed to create such an extraordinary work in the space of a few minutes is remarkable really. It's a work of genius. It's impossible to copy. I'd go so far as to say that it's not just the perfect pop song, it's almost perfect as an idea, existing outside of the song itself. As an idea, "Wichita Lineman" is the most perfect song that's ever been written.

'Why do I love it so much? Because it's not a young man's song, it's a song that develops more and more the older you get, almost like a slowly unfolding photograph. It's a song that you don't grow out of, you grow into. It creeps up on you and never lets go. Also, you can't deny that Glen Campbell looks the part; he looks like the kind of man that would sing this song. It was the right time, right place, right singer, right song. In that respect it's perfect. It seems to exist in a state beyond the usual understanding of recognition. It is somewhat separate from everything around it.'

That's it precisely. 'Wichita' seems to exist in a space of its own, a place of its own, seemingly hovering above the ground, almost in its own bubble. Impervious to seasons, immune to its surroundings, it's like the extra-terrestrial haze in a fifties sci-fi movie, a bit disconcerting at first but actually completely benign.

Sadness is a perennial emotion in music because suffering springs eternal. A morose ballad will not just flatter the songwriter – who will feel as though they are mainlining genuine melancholy, and thus creating actual art – it will flatter the listener, too, as their feelings have in their eyes been validated by a work of great depth. Country Music Hall of Famer Harlan Howard once described country songwriting as 'three chords and the truth', which try to capture universal sentiments. Other writers need to bleed themselves before they can splurge, coming back from the brink with a cunning word about the human condition. In a way, 'Lineman' was the perfect fusion of both, the personal made public, the private writ large.

'I love the song because it's as though it's been in my life for ever,' said the journalist and author Amy Raphael. 'I can't remember where I first heard it – I was only one when it came out – but it always reminds me of my father. It's so cinematic. Completely cinematic.' Or, as Saint Etienne's Bob Stanley said, 'Americana in the truest sense, evocative and hyper-real.'

Someone who knows oceans about the complexity of writing about the human condition, especially the intricacies of domesticity, is Chris Difford, who, among many other wonderful things, is the lyricist in Squeeze. A long-term fan of the song, he is in awe of Webb's songwriting talent, of his ability to create his own language out of the prosaic and the generic. 'His style, both lyrically and musically, is unique,' he said. 'His lyrical threads often don't make sense, you know – the cake left out in the rain, and the Wichita lineman. At first, I thought it was about the train; I didn't know it was about a guy up a telegraph pole. But then I used to think it was a drug-reference song and I was forever trying to find out what the references were. There are certain turns of phrases and certain red herrings that he puts in his lyrics that I think always tripped me up, and I thought he was like an Elvis Costello of his time in a way, a very intelligent use of the English language in an American way. It's a kind of lyrical journey that I was never comfortable with, as I was more comfortable with British lyricism. So, whenever I heard his lyricism, I had to remove myself from the picture somewhat. I just wondered if he was on drugs all the time, and that's what made it special.'

He didn't hear the song until he was in his late twenties, as his musical background 'had a very small iris to it, it was very English'. The only American music he cared for was the absurdity of Frank Zappa and Captain Beefheart and the joy of the Allman Brothers, and much beyond that he didn't really care to venture. 'Then I started to get into James Taylor and Neil Young and all the people that I had missed, the music that had been tabooed when I was young. It was like a second coming, as suddenly I'm bathing in Joni Mitchell and James Taylor and Jimmy Webb songs.

'As for this song, it is very dense, you can't nick from it at all. It's locked in as a song. There's no way of penetrating it or trying to mimic it. It's the imagery that makes the song so special,' he said. 'The fact that he observed a man up a pole, fixing a wire, and made that into a song – something I can only dream of doing – I think that's a gorgeous bit of imagination. I often see people in strange situations in the street and think, "Oh, I'd like to write about that, that would make an interesting song," but I don't think I could do it as much justice as he does, just because of his turn of phrase. It's almost like it was an unfinished language, like the song itself.

'Just take the strings. They could almost be written by Burt Bacharach. They are so melodic and so off the scale they almost grate against the melody of the song. Listening to it, you think, "Oh, I'm not sure about that, but it makes sense." That's what Burt Bacharach does with such style.

'Jimmy Webb was writing domestic stories in a very complicated way. It's like a jigsaw puzzle, trying to understand them. As a lyricist I'm constantly stealing off other writers by listening to the metre, to the idea, to the phrasing and to the emotion, because that's what songwriters do naturally. You simply can't do that with Jimmy Webb, you can't steal from him. You really can't, because it's a story all of itself.'

Difford found 'Wichita Lineman' impressive because he grew up on a fodder of American television and was seduced by the images in the great American pop of the sixties. 'I always thought songwriters in America spoke a different language. Route 66 is an obvious example, because you can't write about the M25 or the A21 in the same way. When I eventually heard the song, I always imagined Glen Campbell performing the song on the back of a horse somewhere in the desert, with a telegraph pole and the sun off in the distance.

'For me, this was all stuff to be dreamt of, but then when I joined a band and went to America, I discovered it actually was there. Hours and hours on a tour bus have taught me that those poles exist and somebody had to put them up, but it took someone to write a song about them, and that's extraordinary in itself. I remember I got a train from Denver to Chicago because I didn't want to fly, and it took three days, the most boring train journey of my life. It was a really uncomfortable trip, in the middle of summer, and the thing that kept going over in my head was, "Somebody made these tracks." So these workers would come from a small town, they would get paid very little to build these tracks, and then eventually they would get on a train and maybe end up in Chicago. So they actually paved their journey for themselves. America is just full of those kinds of dreams.'

It could be argued that the recording is a cleverly constructed composite, made up of Jimmy Webb's words and melody, Glen Campbell's voice, Carol Kaye's talismanic bass line, Al De Lory's strings and the Gulbransen organ. But, Difford said, 'I bet if Jimmy Webb played it on an acoustic guitar it would sound just as mystical. I'm sure it would be spine-chilling. Even though he can't sing it as well and the arrangement wouldn't be there, you would have it in your head because that's what you've grown up with, I think. The seed has already been sown, and you can't get rid of it.'

For Difford, 'Lineman' is probably in his list of the top ten songs ever recorded, although he wouldn't have said that twenty-five years ago. 'I think good songs like that need to breathe, like wine. You need to take the cork out and listen to them quite a few times for them to bed in and to understand the geography of how the song has been created, the landscape of it, if you like. I think, speaking for myself, when I was younger I didn't have the ability to see that, because I was too self-obsessed with being who I was. Once you've got rid of that ego and that cloak, you soak up everything, and I think that's the glorious thing about this song. Now I can listen to it and say, "Oh my god, what a stunning track."'

'"Wichita Lineman" was part of the soundtrack of my childhood – even in an era that was full of great music [the dying days of the sixties], and Webb's love song reached out from the radio and grabbed you by the heart and soul,' said Tony Parsons. 'Although it is totally American, you didn't need to know where Wichita was or what a lineman did (come to think of it, I still don't), but to understand the emotions of the song you did not need to be American, you just needed to be human. And it was a time when popular music had room enough for artists – and Jimmy Webb was an artist, not writing for money or the market, but writing for the ages.

'It would sound great today. It still sounds great today. A love song, but about real love – yearning, longing, aching. Not love fulfilled. Not pop-chart fluff. Not a happy ending. I think the genius of the song is that it places you at the centre of the action. You might not know what a Wichita lineman was, but you knew how he felt.

'It was a song for its time, and for a divided nation, tearing itself apart. It came out when America was on the news every night – the richest land in human history, but desperately unhappy and at war with itself. Jimmy Webb always felt like he was waking up from the American Dream.

'As for Glen Campbell, in a way he was the American equivalent of Jimmy Page, an absolute veteran of the recording studio, a master of session work, completely on top of his craft before he ever stepped into the spotlight. These days talent is thrust raw and blinking into the spotlight. That is why new talent often seems so pitiful and thin these days. Glen Campbell was a great singer, given a song written by a genius.'

In the early nineties, what was previously – and completely pejoratively – called 'easy listening' came back in a major way, at least in the UK. Actually, it's not strictly accurate to say it came back, as it hadn't really been 'here', or indeed anywhere, in the first place. But suddenly it was everywhere – critically acclaimed by respectable critics in music magazines, lauded in newspapers of repute, and played on the radio and in clubs – almost as though it was being re-appreciated because every other form of music had already been resuscitated. Noel Gallagher was gatecrashing gigs by Burt Bacharach, and Austin Powers was a genuine role model. All of the people I had been championing for years, both in public and in private, were now being held up as bastions of great craftsmanship or facilitators of ironic cool. All of a sudden, the writers of children's TV themes from the sixties and seventies were being told that their zippy little ditties had madeleine-like qualities, able to stir the soul like a formative novel, a piece of confectionery or indeed a classic pop single. As everything from heavy metal to rockabilly to northern soul had already been hoiked back on deck, there was literally nothing left to resurrect. After loungecore, which is how it was rebranded, there was nothing else to re-evaluate. Suddenly, simply by standing still I was cool again, or at least my musical taste was. I had all those rare Japanese Burt Bacharach CDs that the music monthlies were now extolling; I had all those Helmut Zacharias singles, courtesy of my parents; and I didn't need a bunch of newly minted loungecore experts to tell me all about the apparently obscure baroque German cousins of John Barry, as I had a West Hampstead basement full of the stuff.

Of course, this reappreciation of the world of Burt Bacharach, John Barry and Glen Campbell didn't last, and after a few years the worm turned again and all anyone appeared to be interested in was the Verve. Not that any of this affected me much. Of course, the commercial aspects of this newfound interest meant that there were now hundreds more CDs of hitherto difficult-to-find vinyl available to buy, and the publicity surrounding this new cottage industry meant that there was a wealth of new information about artists that even I – something of an obsessive – had found it difficult to track down, although there didn't appear to be that many new fellow travellers. People had moved on, leaving me to wallow in a world designed and soundtracked by the likes of Mandingo, Alan Hawkshaw and the Free Design.

This was my happy place, but then it always had been, ever since I was young. Albert Goldman (old muckraker that he was) once said that music was a way for us to keep young, not by trying to stay cool and relevant, but by an almost generational refusal to grow up. To extrapolate, pop stars became surrogate parents, keeping us away from the horrors of growing up and the onslaught of real life.

For me, the horrors of real life had always been at home, being regularly beaten, punched and locked for hours under various staircases in US Air Force quarters, hit so hard by my father I developed a stammer that made it impossible for me to say my own name until I was five years old. If it wasn't me being hit, it was my mother, who was always jumping into her Ford Anglia, disappearing off to see her girlfriend and leaving me to fend for myself, allowing my father to practise more hours of unsupervised torture. Music for me became like Christmas, which was the only time I can remember my parents not fighting, and consequently the only time I can remember not being used as a punchbag by my father. I remember imploring him to stay at home as long as possible after Christmas, in a bid to keep the family unit together for as long as possible, watching daytime TV, making SodaStream cola and pretending that all was right with the world.

And while I would find it easier and easier to find things to be myopic about, it was the world of easy listening that became my haven. Burt. John Barry. Glen Campbell and Jimmy Webb. The three-panel gatefold cover of the Carpenters' 1973 album *Now & Then*, where they're photographed in a newly polished red Ferrari Daytona outside their beautiful suburban tract house in Downey, California? I wanted to live in that picture.

In my own pubescent way, like Glen Campbell and Jimmy Webb, like millions of others, I thought that the West Coast would bring some sort of salvation, some sort of redemption. Could have been Downey, could have been San Bernardino, could have been Hollywood. Actually, could have been anywhere.

I was seventeen when I discovered that there were other people my age who liked 'Wichita' as much as I did. One of the first people I ever met at the Ralph West Halls of Residence – and actually the friend I've known for the longest time – was a fashion student at St Martin's called Corinne Drewery. She came from Lincolnshire but looked as though she'd just stepped out of the time machine that had delivered her – in something of a rush, I'd say – from Carnaby Street in 1966. She wore dresses that could have convincingly been worn by Sandie Shaw, along with all the other accoutrements of Swinging Sixties dress – big plastic earrings (so big they looked like miniature hula hoops), charity-shop shoes and the palest of eye shadows. As I was a surly art-school punk with a leather jacket and a sneer, I think she took me on as a project and sort of forced us to be friends.

Corinne still maintains that when she introduced herself to me in the dining room at the Ralph West, I responded with, 'Please don't talk to me. Please leave me alone and never talk to me again' (or words to that effect). As she was dressed in a pink plastic carrier bag at the time, I think my response was perfectly understandable. But then Corinne really did have the most extraordinary taste in clothes. One day she would come to breakfast wearing a dress made entirely from plastic fly strips, the next she would look like one of the B-52's (although I could make a fairly good case for the B-52's basing their entire look on Corinne). We used to go clubbing together, and I had to suffer the indignity of looking for warehouse parties in yet-to-be-gentrified places like Hoxton and Hackney at three o'clock in the morning, with Corinne looking like one of the Jetsons. One night, as we were on our way to yet another party in the backstreets of King's Cross, we were attacked by a gang of proto-hoodies (casuals they were called back then), and I was stabbed in the head and in the back, cut with a switch-blade razor. Admittedly, I looked like a forties pimp at the time, complete with zoot suit and goatee beard, although my predicament wasn't helped by the fact that Corinne was dressed as a dayglo flowerpot.

We soon discovered we had similar tastes in music, and while she had arrived at her choices via a lifetime spent in the northern soul clubs of Manchester, Blackpool and Wigan – whereas I had arrived at mine via a similar lifetime spent in sweaty pubs nodding along to dodgy prog-rock bands – by the summer of 1977 we liked almost exactly the same old music: classic Motown, Burt Bacharach, Jackie Trent, John Barry and, yes, 'Wichita Lineman'. Because of this, we became fast friends, and as she was a pretty good singer, and as I was a so-so drummer, it wasn't so surprising when we ended up in various bands together. Eventually I decided that I didn't have what it takes to be a professional musician (i.e. talent: I once turned down an offer from Steve Diggle, after he left the Buzzcocks, to be in Flag of Convenience as I knew I couldn't hold a candle to the Buzzcocks' original drummer, John Maher), although Corinne soon forged a more than successful career with Andy Connell (formerly of A Certain Ratio) in Swing Out Sister (a great band with a terrible name), who were formed out of the ashes of the UK electro scene. Back in the eighties, Swing Out Sister had huge hits with songs like 'Breakout', 'Blue Mood' and 'You on My Mind', and in the decades since have released over a dozen extraordinary albums of cool, late-night loungecore (mixed with lashings of urban strings and sixties soul), the sort of music that makes you want to slip on a turtleneck and move to the ski lodge in *On Her Majesty's Secret Service*. Swing Out Sister are, it has to be said, *my kind of thing*. And their album covers always look the same: Corinne's perennially cool bob looming into the frame like the baby in *2001: A Space Odyssey*, and Andy reclining on some retro chaise longue, looking as though he doesn't have a care in the world.

It is always difficult when someone you know writes a book or makes a film or a record or anything remotely creative, as it might be rubbish, and you might hate it. Weirdly, not only did I love Swing Out Sister's music, I've loved everything they've done in the thirty-odd-year period since. Genuinely loved it. In fact, sometimes I think I've loved their music more than they have themselves. Their first LP, 1987's *It's Better to Travel* (another terrible title), contained a clutch bag of hit singles, though it was 1989's euphoric *Kaleidoscope World* which firmly established their loungecore credentials. With such beautiful songs as 'Forever Blue', 'Where in the World' and 'Coney Island Man', the album was a love letter to luxury, a paean to the five-star pop days of yore. 'Coney Island Man' was almost an homage to Bacharach himself, and worthy of inclusion in any great sixties espionage thriller involving a coastline drive (the Riviera, the Santa Monica Freeway, Sorrento, whatever), an implausibly sunny day and a flame-coloured open-top sportscar driven by a wispy blonde in a Jackie O headscarf and Argentine air-hostess sunglasses.

On 'Forever Blue' and another song from the same album, 'Precious Words', the band drew on the talents of Jimmy Webb, and by all accounts he completely transformed them. 'He seemed surprised we wanted to work with him,' said Drewery. 'We had finished the album and cheekily asked if he would arrange two songs, which he did beautifully – they were so good we did instrumental string mixes of the two so you could hear his arrangements in all their glory. He came to Master Rock Studios in Kilburn High Road, and it was amazing to see him at work with a full orchestra, as orchestral musicians are never usually impressed by pop sessions. They seemed somewhat humbled to be working with one of the greats. I offered to make him a cup of tea. When I had left the room, he asked Andy if I would be attending the session. When he told him that I was actually here, and that it was me who was making him the cuppa, he said, "Corinne is making me a cup of tea? Streisand or Sinatra never did that."'

Corinne and Andy met up with Webb in New York a few years after they had worked together and discussed, among many other things, his writing collaborations with the 5th Dimension and Glen Campbell. 'He said what a great and talented guy Glen was to work with, but was keen to point out that they didn't share the same political views,' said Corinne. 'He was so fascinating to talk to. He also told us his kids, who later formed a band, the Webb Brothers, were just starting to make music, and that he had told them to read the complete works of Dylan Thomas before attempting to write a song. It was a great insight into his lyrics, a great insight into "Wichita Lineman".'

The song still crops up in the most unusual places, and in some of the most expected. Instrumental versions can still be heard in the lobbies, cocktail bars and lifts of those hotels that haven't yet been overhauled and turned into mid-century modern theme parks, and it's never surprising to hear it pumping out behind the counter of a sports bar in a small Midwestern airport. A few years ago, I spent a long weekend in New Orleans, caught in a fantastic vortex between Allen Toussaint, Dr John, Tom Jones and (believe it or not) Hugh Laurie, and on my final night, tired but inquisitive, I ventured out into the French Quarter, intent on getting lost, and curious as to whether the historic heart of the city still had the ability to make you feel venturous and tempted. After an evening spent in the kinds of places that seemed to valiantly uphold the city's reputation for the eccentric, the skanky and the sodden, I ended up in what I suppose would be described on TripAdvisor as a vintage heavy-metal gay bar, full of heavily tattooed women (and a few men) who appeared to have an enthusiastic penchant for the likes of Led Zeppelin, Kiss, Deep Purple, AC/DC and Blue Öyster Cult. Perhaps predictably – given the city's inability to be anything other than surprising – after an hour or so of pretty generic weapons-grade HM, whoever was in charge of the playlist did a quick volte-face, and 'Wichita Lineman' came pouring through the PA, causing the enlivened clientele to liven up even more. The DJ had obviously been hitting the local creole absinthe that day, as he followed this with Roy Harper's 'One of Those Days in England' and Television's 'Prove It', immediately making this particular Louisiana heavy-metal gay bar a shoo-in for any best bar in the galaxy competition.

The silhouette of the lineman on the pole is the same today as it was fifty years ago, and while it might seem that the use of cell phones could obviate the need for the telegraph pole, they still transmit electricity. The linemen look the same, too, wearing hi-viz like any other utility worker, but basically the same, still hanging off poles as though they were abseiling down a cliff face. In the summer of 2018, on holiday in Formentera, as I cycled off to the local town I saw a truck ahead of me, a truck full of poles and tubes and reels of wires and boxes and boxes of metal harnesses.

And up in the air, swinging slowly from a pole, were two of them, *trabajadores utilitarios*, bright in their vests, sweating in the thirty-degree dusk but no less attentive. Stupidly, I felt they were an omen, when they were simply going about their work.

Perhaps they were, as three weeks later I met Jimmy Webb in New York, as arranged, to talk to him about his greatest creation.

8: STILL ON THE LINE

Home is a pretty good place to be.

JIMMY WEBB

It's obviously not necessary to meet a person in order to have an opinion about them, or indeed their records, and in some cases it's probably best not to. There are artists whose music I love but whom I don't especially want to meet in case I don't like them, but there are some people you'd fall over yourself to meet. Obviously it's rarely the waifs and strays you want to talk to, it's the bona fide legends. And you want the experience to produce two things: selfishly you want the encounter to give you a greater understanding of their personality (and – a great failing in a journalist, I know – privately you want to like them, too), and professionally you want to walk away with sufficient secrets to build on the established understanding of their work.

I have interviewed enough celebrities to know that, from the moment we meet, there is often a kind of war of attrition between us. Because they are famous they have usually created a self – a self that is not completely them, but curiously is not *not* them either. Which is what the journalist and profile writer Thomas B. Morgan noted back in the mid-sixties: 'Most better-known people tend toward an elegant solution of what they, or their advisors, call "the image problem",' he said. 'Over time, deliberately, they create a public self for the likes of me to interview, observe, and double-check. This self is a tested consumer item of proven value, a sophisticated invention, refined, polished, distilled, and certified OK in scores, perhaps hundreds of engagements with journalists, audiences, friends, family, and lovers. It is the commingling of an image and a personality, or what I've decided to call an Impersonality.'

These days, impersonalities have become so successful that it's nigh on impossible to tell the difference between what is real and what is mediated. Often, because they are always 'on', some celebrities treat their impersonality as their real identity, their real character. And, as a lot of famous people decided long ago that fame was the only way to diminish, if not completely banish, their past, they are completely happy with this.

And, oddly, often we are, too.

I met Jimmy Webb in Wall's Wharf, a large family seafood restaurant right on the water in Bayville that has been serving clams, oysters and fresh seafood to the people of Oyster Bay, on Long Island, for over sixty years. In the summer, you can't move in here, but today, in the middle of October, Webb and I were the only customers. It is the perfect place to interview a man who wrote the quintessential song about the perennial loner. He lives nearby and this is where he comes if he wants a quiet coffee, some uninterrupted CNN or a slow walk along the beach. This part of Long Island, with its yachts and its big dogs and its white clapboard houses, has become something of an enclave for the musical fraternity, and as well as Billy Joel and Jimmy Webb, the late John Barry lived here, just up the road from rock fan John McEnroe and literary recluse Thomas Pynchon (not that anyone ever saw him).

Webb is still a tall man, and he hasn't been diminished by time. He wore a black hoodie, black track pants, a grey T-shirt and charcoal sneakers. He sported an Apple Watch, but would probably hate it if you mentioned this. He was engaging, serious, matter-of-fact and fearsomely bright – not so fearsome that he rams his intellect down your throat, but he's smart. He mostly frowned, in the way that very successful people reserve their smiles for moments that genuinely please them, but when he did smile, you caught a fleeting glimpse of the young Jimmy Webb, the naive song-writer who embraced stardom with an open face and wide-eyed Midwestern wonder. If this was an impersonality, it was certainly one I could work with.

Webb still tours regularly, performing around fifty concerts a year in the US, Australia and Europe. His concerts since Glen Campbell's death have been complicated, however, because he can tell that many of those who come to see him want him to somehow carry Campbell's mantle. He has even been performing some shows with Campbell's daughter, Ashley. 'It's tinged with a kind of bittersweet joy,' said Webb, who admitted the loss of Campbell is still too painful for him to discuss. 'I love doing his music because it keeps Glen's spirit alive. And not to sound too weird about it, I feel Glen around during those performances. I have to ride herd on my emotions when I'm singing because it's just over a year since we lost him and the sense of loss is still very acute and it's very fresh. I can see his face and hear his voice when I'm doing my lame attempts of doing "Wichita Lineman". But all in all, it's a positive experience.

'As long as I'm alive he'll never be forgotten. I will always play Glen Campbell music. I will keep that candle lit. We lost a tremendous talent. And we only scratched the surface of what he was capable of achieving ... I believe in the Greek idea that as long as someone is saying your name, you remain alive. I am keeping his legacy alive. But I also perform because it keeps me alive.'

He is as protective of Campbell as the singer once was of him. 'First of all, we were close. Our families really grew up together, our kids are like best friends. Glen's kids, my kids and Harry Nilsson's kids have all coalesced into this big extended family, and so we are protective of each other. There was a hostile element in the press that pretty much dissed him as a right-wing sort of Establishment character, and by association labelled me as a middle-of-the-road songwriter dotard. And Glen had my back from day one. I wanted – and still strive – to let people know that he was a genius, that he wasn't just an easy-going country boy. I mean, Donald Trump said that one of the reasons he doesn't like the attorney general, Jeff Sessions, is because he has a southern accent, and a southern accent makes him sound stupid. Now, that's coming from a guy who's no Einstein, OK? So, there it is right out in the open, the kind of big-city, intellectual attitude towards people from south of the Mason–Dixon Line: that they are not quite as bright.

'I think Glen should be in the Rock and Roll Hall of Fame. Research is ongoing, but nobody knows how many records he played on, nobody knows. Certainly hundreds, possibly thousands. A friend of mine has got a bunch of Kingston Trio records and he's listening to a song one night called "Desert Pete", and it's a folk tale about a guy who's going across the desert who finds a jug of sparkling water in this hole in the ground, and there's a note from Desert Pete that says, "Drink all the water you can hold, fill the jug and leave it for somebody else." So it's a morality tale. He was listening to it one night and he thought he heard Glen on guitar. And he was right. There's a really hot banjo part in the foreground of the record, shredding it. It's clearly the motor that is driving this record, and I said, "It sure does sound like him to me." We put it on and played it again and we started listening to the harmony, and clear as a bell I could hear Glen's high tenor on the top note of the harmony part. And I said, "Yeah, it's him, because he is singing harmonies." So nobody knows how many of those things are out there. For years there's been this thing called "Nashville Approved", and there's a legend that Glen was always kept off the list because he was so much of a better guitar player than anyone else.'

Jimmy Webb is, fundamentally, good company, an old-fashioned liberal gentleman with exceedingly good manners. We talked for hours, and the only blip was when

I mentioned an old sweetheart. I hadn't expected him to be tetchy, and he wasn't – not until I mentioned Susan Horton, that is, the woman who broke his heart, and the unwitting muse for at least half a dozen of his most famous songs. I mentioned her simply because I wanted to know how she felt about being responsible for some of the most heartbreaking songs ever written. However, my question went down badly, as though I'd just mentioned the one thing I had been warned not to address, like the acrimonious divorce, the ill-judged investment or the never-referred-to brush with the law. Webb looked at me as though all the trust and all the equity that we'd built up together over the last ninety minutes had just evaporated right there in front of us, rising up above the oysters, the scallops and the Cobb salad. But although it briefly created an atmosphere, I was impressed that a scarred heart could still be causing problems over fifty years since it first started to hurt. Wow, this woman had really skewered him, so maybe it was no surprise that the songs were so good. He stopped sipping his coffee for a second and uttered a long, low 'Noooow . . . Was she flattered? Oh, I don't know, what girl wouldn't be flattered? She used to tell me that it kind of embarrassed her, when it was too on point, like "Where's the Playground, Susie?" I don't know how the word got out that it was a real person named Susie Horton, but journalists will be journalists and people started asking me, "Was this a real person?" And I would say, "Yes," and then try to move on. I actually think she became quite proud of the fact, as time went on. But I had it bad. It tore me up pretty badly when she announced that she was getting married. I remember going up to Tahoe and getting her one time. Going up there, she says I kidnapped her, but in this age that we live in, this Me Too movement, I really wish she wouldn't say that because I really didn't, I really didn't kidnap her. I was just ardent. If I kidnapped her, why did she live in my house for two years? She ended up in the sack with my best friend, and that's ultimately why we broke up, and I got rid of him, too.'

He had nothing but good things to say about his most famous song, nothing but good things to say about Glen Campbell, while reserving his ire for the US president and the carelessness of the record industry. He understands that the business has changed, although he's not doing cartwheels.

'Music does change, and it changes into something that you don't want to do. It doesn't change into something that you can't do, because it's childishly simple. Now they are running programs through AI computers that just have the template for a hit record, and they are trying to get computers to write. They are doing this – it's not the ravings of a lunatic. I've been on the board of directors of ASCAP [the American Society of Composers, Authors and Publishers] for over twenty years, ever since Napster, from the bitter beginnings of this whole depredation that has been perpetrated by digital interests to devalue copyright and to really put us out of a job. Because they don't want to have to deal with people, it's easier just to have a room full of servers to write the music. They don't have any chords, they don't have any melodies, they don't have any lyrics. Those are all the things that I'm interested in – I mean, incredibly interested in. Totally absorbed with, dedicated, in the deepest part of my being. I'm a creature that just deals with chords, melody and halfway decent lyrics.'

On 8 August 2017, Glen Campbell eventually succumbed to Alzheimer's disease, in Nashville, his adopted spiritual home, aged eighty-one. In 2011, the year of his diagnosis, he released the album *Ghost on the Canvas* and announced that he would continue with his planned shows, regardless of his illness. Inevitably, the tour turned into a long goodbye, and the original five-week run turned into a marathon that included 151 shows in fifteen months.

'I don't know anything about it because I don't feel any different,' he said at the time. 'The stuff I can't remember is great because it's a lot of stuff I don't want to remember anyway. Does it get harder breathing new life into those old songs? No, every night is different. I got to know Sinatra quite well, and that's what he tried to do. Every song was a unique performance. I still love "Gentle on My Mind", and "By the Time I Get to Phoenix" still makes me real homesick. I've been very lucky in my career. For my whole life I felt like I was at the right place at the right time. It seemed like fate was always leading me to the right door.'

Campbell was post-rehab golfing buddies with Alice Cooper, and they used to play together regularly when they weren't on tour. ('He was a master short game player,' said Cooper. 'The best I ever played with.') Cooper knew something was wrong with his friend when he started repeating himself on the golf course, telling him a joke when they teed off, and then telling it again at least twice before the end of the round. 'That's when I knew something was up,' said Cooper. 'But give him a guitar and he was a virtuoso.'

'I didn't care for golf,' said Webb, 'and I wouldn't be caught dead with a golf club in my hand, unless there was a very poisonous reptile nearby. Glen bought me a set of golf clubs once. He'd say, "How you getting on with the clubs?" "Not so good, Glen..." He was an Orange County Republican. It's a snotty thing to say, but they were around back then, and that's what we called them. Bob Hope. John Wayne. The enablers of the Vietnam War mentality. John Wayne mixing with the Green Berets. Bob Hope going over there to rouse them. Sending out this signal that we're winning this thing...'

When Campbell died, there were eulogies for months. 'He had a beautiful singing voice,' said Bruce Springsteen. 'Pure tone. And it was never fancy. Wasn't singing all over the place. It was simple on the surface but there was a world of emotion underneath.' A few years beforehand, Amanda Petrusich wrote this lovely reminiscence in the *New Yorker*: 'I met Campbell once, at the Nashville airport. All of my belongings (including my laptop, which contained an early and otherwise unsaved draft of a magazine feature I'd spent months reporting) had recently been stolen from my rental car. It was parked in a garage downtown; one of its rear windows had been smashed in with a rock. During the ensuing hubbub – phoning the cops, explaining the compromised state of my Kia Sephia to the rental-car agency – my flight back to New York City had departed without me. I was consoling myself by drinking a great deal of beer at an outpost of Tootsie's Orchid Lounge, the famed Broadway honky-tonk. This must have been in 2009.

'I looked up and saw Campbell wandering around with his wife, Kim Woollen. (They'd met on a blind date – he took her to dinner at the Waldorf-Astoria, with his parents, and then to a James Taylor concert.) Campbell hadn't been diagnosed with Alzheimer's yet, not in any official capacity, but it was clear, even then, that he wasn't quite himself – that certain ideas or bits of language were receding, drifting out of reach, like paper boats fluttering across a pond.

'I approached and brazenly asked for a photograph – I suppose I felt like I had little left to lose in Nashville that afternoon. They were so gracious. You know, it wasn't that bad, losing my stuff and missing my flight. There would be more stuff, more flights. He threw a big arm around me and we grinned.'

Jimmy Webb was in close contact with Campbell during those final years, and he said that towards the end just about the only coherent phrases Campbell could muster were song lyrics, presumably through muscle memory. It broke his heart to see his friend this way, but he didn't see how he could not visit him. After all, they had spent a lifetime together, on and off. 'They'll remember a song after everything else is gone,' he told me. 'They'll remember the lyrics. They'll remember the melody. They'll be staring out the window blankly. Then they'll burst into song.'

The day Campbell died, Webb released a statement, some of which is here:

Let the world note that a great American influence on pop music, the American Beatle, the secret link between so many artists and records that we can only marvel, has passed and cannot be replaced. He was bountiful. His was a world of gifts freely exchanged: Roger Miller stories, songs from the best writers, an old Merle Haggard record or a pocket knife.

He gave me a great wide lens through which to look at music. The cult of The Players? He was at the very centre. He loved the Beach Boys and in subtle ways helped mould their sound. He loved Don and Phil [Everly], Bill Medley and Bobby Hatfield, Flatt and Scruggs. This was the one great lesson that I learned from him as a kid: Musically speaking nothing is out of bounds.

One of his favourite songs was 'Try A Little Kindness' in which he sings 'shine your light on everyone you see'. My God. Did he do that or what? When it came to friendship Glen was the real deal. He spoke my name from ten thousand stages. He was my big brother, my protector, my co-culprit, my John

255

crying in the wilderness. Nobody liked a Jimmy Webb
song as much as Glen!

Jimmy

For over fifty years, Jimmy Webb has been dealing in
crushed broken hearts, with his songs acting like road maps,
route maps, lovingly drawn directions to somewhere where
life is better. In Webb's heart, everything is a picture. 'When
I think about those days, the only way I can imagine them
is sort of with a picture. I can see a house by a road. That's
the only way I can recall it.'

He holds his most famous song in great affection, and
while he occasionally says that he won't perform it again,
he always does, even more so now that Glen Campbell has
passed. He has told the story of its birth so many times now
that it has taken on a life of its own, folded into a kind of
parallel narrative. Today, however, on Long Island's North
Shore, in search of a definitive version he stopped to analyse
every well-worn anecdote, every half-truth, every automatic response.

'I suppose the story is this,' he said, with as much care
as he could muster. 'It was written about the Oklahoma
Panhandle, which was really the Cherokee strip [the
sixty-mile stretch of land south of the Oklahoma–Kansas
border], where the Cherokee lived until we decided we
would take that away from them, because that's what we
did. We gave them things and then took them away again.
This area is completely flat, and at the western end is New

Mexico, the badlands, and to the south is West Texas, and it's all pretty much desert. [In 1966, Truman Capote's *In Cold Blood* was published by Random House, its opening sentence reflecting much about how Kansans, inhabiting one of the most lonesome places in the country, saw themselves.] There's this little town right at the western end of the Panhandle called Boise City, and they say you can stand in Boise City and see into New Mexico, which is about fifty miles away, so the land really falls off. There's this huge distance, and it is very desolate. There is an occasional hog farm or maybe small dwelling, nothing you would recognise as anything other than very, very small towns. The rest of it is almost like a scene out of a fifties western, with a wagon train going out across the plains. The only thing that's visible is these telegraph poles and the wires between them. It's so remote and it's so quiet, with no one moving, that you can actually pull your car up by the side of the road, which my father actually did for me one day and said, "Come with me and listen." And he walked with me under the lines, under the wires, and they were singing. They were actually making this musical sound, out there in the middle of nowhere. Electricity actually makes noise as it's going through the wires, which is a little bit insane when you think about it, but it does make a noise if you're in a place where it's quiet. Whether it's the resistance of the wires and the electricity overcoming that as it pushes through . . . It's a frequency modulation of some kind.

'We would drive along these roads and see these guys out there, with their truck parked, and there's not a soul around for ten, fifteen, twenty-five miles. There's not a soul moving, except for hawks and little rabbits and things like that. Creatures of the plains. You'd see the occasional automobile, so what I was after in the song, I was after that sort of loneliness. It really goes hand in hand with the idea that it's so quiet out there that you can hear the wires making this noise.

'I think it's fine that I didn't finish it, because I don't think it would have been as clean as it was, or as minimalist. It was sort of caught before any extraneous rococo could be added to it. It was sort of jerked out of the creative process and hot off the press. So there is a very minimalist quality to that record that complements the image of the high-wire guy, the lineman. His loneliness is this solitude that I witnessed first-hand.

'Technically, I suppose the song is about the point where the Midwest meets the West. This is where the Santa Fe Trail used to head out for California, and you can still see the ruts out there of the wagons. So really, this is kind of the West and New Mexico, which is where all the outlaws went after they robbed the banks, you know. There was a lot of shooting and a lot of outlaws and stuff going on in Missouri and Oklahoma, and we refer to that whole genre as westerns, but you are right, it's smack dab in the middle of the country. But it was a different time, when the West was closer to the centre of the country. As America expanded and more people moved west, so our idea of the West kept being pushed closer to the coast.

'My family actually started in Virginia. Long ago, I traced my genealogy, using a Mormon genealogist out of Salt Lake City. I traced our family back through Alabama to Georgia to Virginia at the time of the Revolution, so when I look back at my DNA, I'm 61 per cent Irish. There is such a big fear of immigration in the country right now, but I wouldn't be here if it wasn't for immigration, and my family have been here for two hundred years. This administration very conveniently forgets that every square foot of America was taken from someone by force, lethal force and cruelty beyond imagination. It isn't like God prepared America for his special people, who came over and were white, but there are people here who sort of think that's the way it happened. Every square foot, someone died for. Probably a brown person. Texas was stolen from the Spanish, California was stolen from the Spanish. If you read our history books, that's not what you read. You read that there were wars, but they were predations by the Indians on the peaceful settlers. They gave them black hills in Dakota – for as long as the rivers run and as long as the sky is blue, as long as the hawk flies – until some knuckleheads found gold up in the hills, and then Custer was sent in there to drive them out.

'So I sort of recognise my place in westward expansion. My genealogist said one time that the churchyards of Georgia are full of Webbs. "If you ever want to see your ancestors, go to Georgia," he said. And in the Civil War, we were on the wrong side – my family were wearing grey. And so, when the family got to Oklahoma, little Jimmy was born. I was raised down in the south-west of Oklahoma and moved to West Texas, which was a hotbed for the whole rock and roll thing. I was a big Buddy Holly fan and soon decided I wanted to be a songwriter.'

And then he brought out that huge Midwestern smile, before settling on an even bigger Midwestern frown.

'There's lots of Wichitas. If you look at a map of the Midwest, there is a Wichita, Kansas, a Wichita, Oklahoma, there's a Wichita, Texas. There's also very prominently a Wichita River, and the battle of the Wichita River was a massacre. George Armstrong Custer rode in at dawn on a defenceless village. All the men were out hunting; it was winter. Every living thing – every woman, every child, every fucking dog – he killed everything that moved in that village, and the army had the temerity to call it the battle of the Wichita rather than the massacre at Wichita. But in my mind I decided that's where it was – in Wichita, in Kansas. The song was about many places in the area, but it's set in Wichita, Kansas. That's it.'

He stopped for a while to consider again how he felt when he wrote it, and a thought occurred to him, one he couldn't remember having before. 'Maybe for a while it was "Arkansas Lineman", but who knows? The way I work, I'm moving so fast that unless I had my notes, unless I had actually the pieces of paper that I had on the piano that day, I couldn't say whether it was originally "Arkansas Lineman". I never went through that because it was like releasing an arrow.

'These days it takes me a lot longer to write a song, because you get to the point where you measure everything. Once you realise you are going to be judged on everything, you measure everything. You go, "Do I really want to use that word? How is that going to play?" you know? "Do I really have the right wires on top of this telephone pole?" Because when I wrote the song, I didn't know; I didn't know that much about the technicalities of being a lineman.'

While the Oklahoma Panhandle might be short of land-marks, it is not short of history, a no-man's-land that no state wanted, a haven for outlaws and vigilantes. It still feels a little like that, and the roads here are no different today to how they were in 1968. As you drive west along Highway 412 – a relatively recent addition to the highway system – for instance, the road really does go on for ever. I needed to see for myself, and when I did, I wasn't disappointed. To look at these roads, these poles, this sky, it's easy to think that nothing much has changed in the fifty years since Jimmy Webb wrote about them. It's the same on the dirt roads. In this part of the country, in this sacramental place, all you can really see is sky, as the floor below is almost inciden-tal, a wide yellow mass of scrub broken only by hundreds, thousands of telegraph poles. There is simply nothing here, only distance, and the sensation of being completely alone. It's unsettling, but also strangely empowering. Out here, in the mythical, physical West, your only friend is the radio, your only respite from heat, sky and memory. Driving out here is not so dissimilar from driving along Route 66, where it's easy to imagine yourself hauled back in time to a place before the Interstates, when the only way to get from A to B was to start early. It is desolate. Sure, it is romantic and gives you a sense of existential ennui, but mainly it is desolate. There is wheat, and there is tumbleweed, and there is tarmac. And sky and poles and not much else. People have compared the experience of driving along these long stretches of road to being in a sensory deprivation tank, with nothing to see, smell, feel or hear, and at times the landscape can overwhelm you, almost becoming abstract as the miles keep building. The thing that keeps you going is the horizon, the never-changing, unforgiving horizon. Today that horizon is littered with wind turbines, which can make the telegraph poles that still flank the old routes look a little like old men staggering towards the county line, looking for home, rolling like crucifixes westward towards the coast, stoic and metronomic.

As ineffably joyful journeys go, the drive through Oklahoma is one of the best, as well as one of the longest, the roads snaking their way through one dustbowl town after another, concrete and asphalt ribbons down which millions of tourists once pushed their Detroit steel, looking for the new world or simply the definitive road experience. On the extraordinarily evocative drive west from Boise City to Guymon on Route 64, it's not difficult to picture in one's mind the hard times described in John Steinbeck's *The Grapes of Wrath*. Towns out here finish before they begin, fading into scrub. These are moonscapes of monstrous proportions, with two-lane blacktops cutting through them like charcoal arrows. To drive on Route 64 or Route 66, which runs parallel to the south, is to step back in time, to relive an age when driving was still an adventure, not a necessity. After World War II, when the car was still king, these roads that had once been the service roads to California became the stuff of fantasy. The country towards the west of Oklahoma can make you feel light-headed with solitude – creviced arroyos, harsh desert and wild bush scrub. 'Sometimes, toward either end of a long driving day,' wrote Tom Snyder in one of his roadside companions, 'a run through this country brings up an ancient German word, *Sehnsucht*. It has no equivalent in English, but it represents a longing for, a need to return to, a place you've never been.'

It is a sensation that springs to mind when thinking about 'Wichita Lineman'.

Here, in western Oklahoma, as the late afternoon starts to fold into the evening, and as shadow begins to add some context to the landscape, any feelings of deprivation – sensorial or emotional – are banished, as the sky takes over, morphing into a kaleidoscopic canopy.

The only constant is the telegraph poles, a glissando to the sea . . .

There are so many pictures in Jimmy Webb's life, pictures that trace the career of a man who caught fame early and who mirrored its well-worn narrative arc before coming out the other side with a reputation the size of Mount Rushmore. Glen Campbell, too, had the same pictures, the ones of him as confident young buck who became so successful he even – for one year only, in 1968 – outsold the Beatles, before succumbing to those hoary old clichés of wine, women and dope. He, too, can still be seen on YouTube, pumping out his classic hits in his rehab years, wiser and with a stronger voice than ever.

Most of these pictures are good for both of them, although the images we like the best are the ones of them in their prime, in their pomp, when the world was at their feet and when their songs had found their way into our hearts for the very first time. We might not have fallen in love with 'Wichita Lineman' until the seventies, the nineties, the noughties, whenever; and we might not have fallen in love with it until last week, but we fell in love with it in its infancy. We love hearing Glen Campbell sing the original, and we love watching him sing it most when it was released, in 1968, when he was thirty-two and Jimmy Webb was still only twenty-one. The strongest image we have of Webb is the one where he sits cross-legged in his white turtleneck sweater, his white jeans and his little white boots. He has a Beatle cut, a hint of stubble, and wears an expression that could be sufficiently described as sanguine.

The image many love of Glen Campbell, or at least the one I love, is a still from his appearance on *The Smothers Brothers Comedy Hour* in 1968, where he performs 'Wichita

Lineman' against a set composed largely of huge, angular telegraph poles that look as though they have been designed by Saul Bass. A sunset has been painted approximately on the backdrop. Campbell stands with one foot against the base of a pole, strumming what looks like a Fender Bass VI and smiling over the top of the camera, looking as though he's peering up into the sky, forty feet above the ground perhaps. He's wearing a modish brown suit, ankle boots and a pale-yellow roll-neck, perfectly groomed but also having the appearance of someone who has quite literally just walked in off the street.

Then, as the song reaches one minute and twenty seconds, he turns and looks directly into the camera, his matinee parting and the cleft in his chin telling you he means business. Show business. This was Glen Campbell's face for the world to see. And maybe Jimmy Webb's, too. Campbell blinks, feeling rangy and freewheeling, and then he drops the bomb, the bomb that never stops: 'And I need you more than want you / and I want you for all time . . .' And in the mind's eye, the telegraph poles appeared to be flashing by in rhythm.

Having both taken a metaphorical trip along Route 66 to find fame and fortune, their greatest success would be an anthem celebrating the Midwest, the place where both of them were born.

Unsurprisingly, of all the recordings that Campbell made of Webb's songs, 'Wichita Lineman' remains Webb's favourite. 'It was a perfect marriage between a song and a voice,'

he said. 'It's amazing today to listen to that record and realise how highly pitched his voice is, because all of our voices
have dropped in the intervening years. But he sung so high
and he was such a smooth singer, and there was a note – it
was very plaintive, almost like a dying fall – to his intona-
tion, to things that are almost indescribable, almost intangible. But I don't think that the record has lost any gravitas
since it was made. You put it on and it still sounds as though
that song and that singer were meant to be together.

'Over the years I've changed my mind a little bit about
"Wichita Lineman", as I've realised it must be better than
I thought it was, but I always come back to the fact that I
didn't finish it. If I had finished it, it wouldn't have been
as clean. Because it was kind of an interrupted creative
process, because Al De Lory wrote a sort of precognitive
arrangement, and it was almost childishly simple. He was
a minimalist before his time, before its time, and you can
hear it on "Wichita Lineman". Glen also has the perfect
instrument for that song; it was absolutely written for his
voice, and I knew exactly where his voice was on the piano.
"Wichita Lineman" stands up as a record, it still sounds
great. If it came on the jukebox right now in this place' – he
looked around the empty Wall's Wharf bar – 'bam! There is
an immediate identification of that sound, that voice. There
is a pairing between the song and the voice. I attribute a lot
of its longevity to that, because it's not really coloured by
any particular era, just it's a phenomenal record. The record
is like a Picasso line drawing. I can say that because I didn't

make the record besides holding down the two notes on the church organ. They made the record, and Glen knew how to make records. He'd already made thousands of records. He had played on "Viva Las Vegas" with Elvis Presley, he'd done "You've Lost That Loving Feelin'", he played on "Johnny Angel". The depth of his knowledge of what to do in the studio, you can't count that out. You can't disregard that as a factor.

'He came over to my house one day to watch a football game, and I put a record on that I had been toying with, by Allen Toussaint. I said, "Listen to this guy." Some of his stuff was pretty far out; it was borderline, sort of psyche-delic in a way. We finally came to "Southern Nights", and he listened to it and with kind of a glazed look over him – he forgot all about the game – he said, "Can I have that?" And I said, "Don't ask me, it's Al Toussaint's, it's already recorded." And he says, "No, can I have that record?" I said, "Well, I'm not really finished with it, but I guess so." He grabbed it, and it was like a Warner Brothers cartoon – he went out the door like boom, like the coyote. Then a couple of weeks later it came on the radio, his version of "Southern Nights", and it was a huge hit. Glen completely took it apart and put it back together again, and when he got finished with it, man, there was no doubt: when it came into a radio station it was going onto the turntable.

'I have a kind of angst against people who try to diminish Glen as being any less of a musician than he was, any less of an intellect than he was. He was a record man, through and through, and he came up with those session players, the Wrecking Crew, so he had already sat through a hundred thousand sessions where they didn't cut any hits, so he sort of knows what an un-hit sounds like. I gave him all the credit in the world for "Wichita Lineman". He knew it was finished. Whether I knew it was finished or not, he knew it was finished.'

Call it a working-man blues, call it a hymn, call it people music, call it whatever you want. The beauty of 'Wichita Lineman', like the constant retelling of how Jimmy Webb came to write it, is in the repetition. 'I've never worked with high-tension wires or anything like that,' he said. 'My characters were all ordinary guys. They were all blue-collar guys who did ordinary jobs. And they came from ordinary towns. They came from places like Galveston and Wichita and places like that.

'No, I never worked for the phone company. But then, I'm not a journalist. I'm not Woody Guthrie, I'm a songwriter, and I can write about anything I want to. I feel that you should know something about what you're doing, and you should have an image, and I have a very specific image of a guy I saw working up on the wires out in the Oklahoma Panhandle one time with a telephone in his hand talking to somebody. And this exquisite aesthetic balance of all these telephone poles just decreasing in size as they got further and further away from the viewer – that being me – and as I passed him, he began to diminish in size. The country is so flat, it was like this one quick snapshot of this guy rigged up on a pole with this telephone in his hand. And this song came about, really, from wondering what that was like, what it would be like to be working up on a telephone pole, and what would you be talking about? Was he talking to his girlfriend? Probably just doing one of those checks where they called up and said, "Mile marker 46," you know? "Everything's working so far.'"

Everything's still working now.

ACKNOWLEDGEMENTS

When I told members of my immediate family I was writing a book about 'Wichita Lineman', they pretty much all said the same thing: 'That's nice. Why?' (although Jimmy Webb himself was just as incredulous when I told him the same thing). Hopefully this book goes some way to answering that question. As well as thanking Sarah, Edie and Georgia, I'd like to thank all the people who helped with the book, for their enthusiasm, their contributions, their wise words, their suggestions and their expertise. So, a huge hearty round of applause please to Jimmy Webb, Carol Kaye, Laura Savini, Lee Brackstone, Jonny Geller, Anne Owen, Ian Bahrami, Paul Weller, Chris Difford, Elvis Costello, Jon Savage, Corinne Drewery, Tony Parsons, Robert Chalmers, Mick Brown, Deyan Sudjic, Dan Papps, Jo Vickers, the Mark Hotel, Linda Ronstadt, Bill Prince, Andrew Collins, Stuart Maconie, Mark Ellen, Neil McCormick, Rod Melvin, Robin Derrick, Robert Elms, Alex James, Mark Steyn, David Hepworth, Barney Hoskyns, Jason Barlow, Amy Raphael, Bob Stanley and Doug Flett. There are so many sources for the research and quotes used in this book, and the following publications have been incredibly helpful: *Billboard*, *Country Music Review*, *Daily Express*, *Daily Mail*, *Daily Telegraph*, *Esquire*, *Evening Standard*, *The Face*, *Financial*

Times, British *GQ*, *Guardian*, *Independent*, *Independent on Sunday*, *Los Angeles Times*, *Mail on Sunday*, *Melody Maker*, *Mojo*, *Music Week*, *New Musical Express*, *New York Post*, *New York Review of Books*, *New York Times*, *New Yorker*, *Observer*, *Q*, *Record Mirror*, *Rolling Stone*, *Scotland on Sunday*, *Scotsman*, *Sounds*, *Sunday Express*, *Sunday Telegraph*, *Sunday Times*, *The Times*, *Uncut*, *Vanity Fair* and *Washington Post*. I have also raided the top and bottom drawers of dozens of websites, Wikipedia and Wikiquotes included, many of which are extraordinary in their obsession with detail. Rock's Backpages has also been extremely helpful.

BIBLIOGRAPHY

Amis, Martin, *The Moronic Inferno* (Jonathan Cape, 1986)

Bull, Andy, *Coast to Coast* (Black Swan, 1993)

Campbell, Debby and Mark Bego, *Glen Campbell: Life with My Father* (Omnibus, 2014)

Campbell, Glen with Tom Carter, *Rhinestone Cowboy: An Autobiography* (Villard Books, 1994)

Canfield, Jack, Mark Victor Hansen and Randy Rudder, *Chicken Soup for the Soul: Country Music* (Simon & Schuster, 2011)

Dimery, Robert (ed.), *1001 Songs You Must Hear Before You Die* (Cassell Illustrated, 2010)

Granata, Charles L., *I Just Wasn't Made for These Times: Brian Wilson and the Making of* Pet Sounds (Unanimous, 2003)

Hartman, Kent, *The Wrecking Crew: The Inside Story of Rock and Roll's Best-Kept Secret* (Thomas Dunne, 2012)

Herr, Michael and Guy Peellaert, *The Big Room* (Picador, 1986)

James, Alex, *A Bit of a Blur* (Little, Brown, 2007)

Jones, Dylan, *The Biographical Dictionary of Popular Music* (Bedford Square Books, 2012)

Jones, Dylan, *Elvis Has Left the Building: The Day the King Died* (Duckworth Overlook, 2014)

Kaye, Carol, *Studio Musician: Carol Kaye, 60s No. 1 Hit Bassist, Guitarist* (Burbank Printing, 2017)

Lewis, Michael, *The Fifth Risk* (Allen Lane, 2018)

Peel, John, *Margrave of the Marshes* (Bantam, 2005)

Ronstadt, Linda, *Simple Dreams: A Musical Memoir* (Simon & Schuster, 2013)

Stimeling, Travis D., *The Country Music Reader* (Oxford University Press, 2014)

Walker, Michael, *Laurel Canyon* (Faber & Faber, 2006)

Webb, Jimmy, *The Cake and the Rain* (St. Martin's Press, 2017)

Webb, Jimmy, *Tunesmith: Inside the Art of Songwriting* (Hyperion, 1998)

Zollo, Paul, *Songwriters on Songwriting* (Da Capo, 2003)

IMAGE CREDITS